An Actor Adrift

YOSHI OIDA
with Lorna Marshall

Foreword by PETER BROOK

Methuen Drama

This book was written in collaboration with Lorna Marshall,
a director and teacher of theatre based in London.

Methuen Drama

10 9 8 7 6 5

First published in the United Kingdom in 1992 by Methuen London

Methuen Drama
A & C Black Publishers
36 Soho Square
London W1D 3QY

www.methuendrama.com

A CIP catalogue record for this book is available from the British
Library

ISBN 978 0 413 65840 1

Typeset by Wilmaset Ltd, Birkenhead, Wirral
Printed and bound in Great Britain by
CPI Antony Rowe, Chippenham and Eastbourne

An Actor Adrift

To Hugh McCormick,
who no longer exists

Contents

List of illustrations

Foreword
by Peter Brook

'You are going to meet an actor from the Noh theatre,' Jean-Louis Barrault told me. The door in his office opened and in place of the impressive figure in a kimono that I half-expected to see, the man who entered was quite small, dressed in a formal suit and tie. He knew no English, no French, but he expressed himself in another way. He bowed, he bowed again and again, I felt I understood and when I asked him to be part of our first International Workshop, Yoshi bowed in agreement. The first day, some twenty actors and actresses from different countries gathered together and in order to break the ice and establish an informal atmosphere we sat on the ground. As my muscles were stiff I gave myself a cushion and Yoshi sat opposite me, perfectly poised in lotus position. After a while, I shifted uncomfortably and leaned on one arm. To my surprise Yoshi did likewise. By the end of the day, I was sprawling on my elbows and saw a very unhappy Yoshi lying flat on the ground. Many weeks later, I asked him whether he enjoyed lying down from time to time. 'Not at all,' he answered. 'But you are the teacher. From childhood in Japan we learn that the pupil must be lower than the teacher. I had no choice.'

Since then, many things have changed. Yoshi is a comrade, a friend and always a teacher in his own right. We have lived through many adventures together and I find it hard to conceive of exploring any new territory without Yoshi, always ready to lead, to guide or to follow as the occasion demands, with a talent and a skill that were formed by Japan but which are essentially his own.

Even today people frequently ask me 'Why an International group?' 'What use is it for people from different cultures to try to work together?' 'Is it possible?' Yoshi's book in which he links his search as an actor to his search for meaning in his life illuminates these questions through his own personal experience.

One day Yoshi told me of the saying of an old Kabuki actor: 'I can teach a young actor the movement of how to point to the moon. But from his finger-tip to the moon, that's the actor's responsibility.' And Yoshi added: 'When I act, what matters is not whether my gesture is beautiful. For me, there is only one question. Did the audience see the moon?'

With Yoshi, I have seen many moons.

Paris, 1992

Introduction

Sometimes I wake up in the middle of the night and find myself completely lost. I feel as if I have been thrown into space, floating about without a physical body. At these moments, I am seized by basic fears and questions. Is this place dangerous? 'Where exactly am I?'

I struggle back to consciousness. I begin to register noises and notice things around me. I remember where I am sleeping. The place could be anywhere from the sleeping car in an Indian night train, to a folding camp bed under the stars at the edge of an African village. Then my sense of smell starts to return. Each place has its own distinct perfume. A special Indian scent for India, an Arabian one for the desert lands, the characteristic odour of Paris.

Reassured by all these sounds, sights and smells, I start to position myself on an imaginary globe in my head. This makes me happier about my place in the world. But the map in my head is not the map I grew up with in Tokyo, which has Japan as the centre of the world. That map has America to the right, lying beyond the Pacific Ocean, with New York on the far right hand side. Left of Japan is China and India, then Europe, and finally London, clinging to the margin of the page. The map I wake up to now is the Western one, where the centre is Europe, and Japan is barely visible in the upper right hand corner. It really is

1

the 'Far East', and Japan is merely a collection of small islands at the very edge of the world.

And now I can place myself, somewhere outside Japan. But the feeling of floating in space still persists, and triggers another sort of anxiety. Nothing outside this bed has any relation to me. Why am I alone in this place? Why am I sleeping here? What am I, having no home, no family, drifting around like a piece of seaweed, at my age?

Outside large cities, children point their fingers at me, shouting, 'A Chinaman, a Chinaman!' I don't understand why I should be treated like this, just because I have an oriental face. Even adults sometimes react in this way. Occasionally, when I try to order a drink in a bar, I may be told that the place is already closed. In other areas, with a lot of Japanese tourists, people treat you as a guest, but even there, as soon as you try to settle down, it is an entirely different story. The only time I am truly treated as an equal is when I am directing, or acting on stage. Perhaps if you are a master of karate, you may enjoy special consideration and privileges, but the average Japanese foreigner remains an outsider.

Quite often my Japanese actor friends visit me at my home in Paris and compliment me, saying, 'You are very brave, working with foreigners, in an environment so different to home.'

And my usual reply is: 'On the contrary, you are the one that is brave: still bearing up under the pressure of a closely-knit society, being stabbed in the back by certain people in the narrow theatrical circle, and generally worrying about your situation. Yet through all this, you still keep on working. I could never have had such courage. I am a coward, and so I chose to run away from Japan and work abroad with strangers. In reality, I could be described as one of "society's rejects"!'

I meet other Japanese living in Paris, who say, 'I have wound up all my affairs in Japan. I am going to bury my bones in France.'

2

For me it is different. I do not want to die here. I don't mind drifting aimlessly round the world, but I still wish to die in Japan. In the Osaka area where I was born, to be exact. I cannot really explain this feeling, but I know this is how I want to end my life.

Of course, when I left Japan, I had no idea that the question of where I planned to die would arise. My initial departure was in April 1968, in the midst of the student protest movement.

It began with a phone call from the actress, Teruko Nagaoka. She asked me if I would be interested in going to Paris. The Professor of French Literature, Rikie Suzuki, had contacted her about a letter he had just received from Jean-Louis Barrault, asking him to recommend a Japanese actor. At that time, Jean-Louis Barrault was the Director of the Odéon Theatre in Paris. Every year he organised a festival of international theatre at the Odéon, called the 'Théâtre des Nations'. For the 1968 festival he decided to invite Peter Brook, who was then a director with the Royal Shakespeare Company. Brook planned to do an experimental version of *The Tempest*, mixing American, French and Japanese actors. They originally wanted to invite Hisao Kanze from the Noh theatre, or Mansaku Nomura from Kyogen, but their schedules were already full. They certainly couldn't leave Japan for as long a period as two months at such short notice. After they had declined, Professor Suzuki approached me to see whether I would be interested. Although I was mainly known as a Western-style actor, through my work in films and theatre, he felt that I would be suitable for this project since I had also studied traditional Noh theatre and Bunraku-style storytelling.

At that time, Peter Brook's name was virtually unknown to the Japanese. But Professor Suzuki guaranteed that if Barrault was producing the project, it would be financially sound. And so I thought, 'If the worst comes to the worst, at least I'll have a free sightseeing tour.'

Like most Japanese at that time, I had no clear idea about the West. For most of its history, Japan had remained isolated from

3

foreign influences, and it had only opened itself to trade and new ideas in the late nineteenth century. Since then, Japan has actively incorporated many Western elements into its industry and society, and this has created a superficial impression of 'Westernisation'. But these 'Western' elements have been viewed with some ambivalence by the people, and in many cases have been changed into 'Japanese versions'. In addition, the average Japanese person had not travelled overseas or even met a European until very recently. The idea of visiting Europe was strange and exciting, but also a little bit worrying. I had no real idea of what I would encounter. Nonetheless, I decided to go.

Unfortunately, it wasn't that easy to arrange. I was in a television Samurai series, and was performing in a play in the evenings. In addition, I was rehearsing for two other productions. I asked the television company to change the story so that my character could disappear, and the understudy took over my part in the play. There were only twenty days before my scheduled departure, and so I had no time to prepare myself or learn English. I was very worried about that, since I have absolutely no talent for languages. (In order to graduate from Keio University, I even had to take a supplementary English exam.) Another thing that made me apprehensive at that time was the fact that many actors working in modern Japanese theatre were trying to imitate Europeans. The thought of acting alongside Europeans made me feel like a student trying to play on the same stage as his teacher.

I took these worries to a friend, Tadashi Iizawa, and asked for his advice. He said: 'There is no need for concern. You have trained in Kyogen and Gidaiyu, which are unknown to foreign actors. Wear traditional costume and go as a Japanese actor. Never, never, under any circumstances, mention that you have played Hamlet. They will laugh at you.'

In fact, I had never played Hamlet, but his comment made me think, and I saw his point. If an American actor came to Japan,

4

and said he had performed a major role in a Kabuki play, he would not be taken seriously by Japanese actors. However, his other suggestion (that I wear a kimono) seemed a bit extreme. I knew the writer Yukio Mishima, and I decided to consult him about this. He agreed with my friend, saying, 'Unfortunately, this is the image of Japan that foreigners have.'

The formal kimono worn in actual performances is made of silk, and often worn with heavy over-trousers called 'hakama'. Since this outfit is both fragile and expensive, actors generally wear a light cotton kimono, called a 'yukata', for rehearsals. Since I was quite used to performing in traditional costume, and it was normal for me to rehearse in a yukata, I decided to take these outfits to Paris. After all, was it right to wear a tracksuit simply in order to imitate European actors?

I had studied Kyogen, a style of comic play traditionally performed in conjunction with Noh theatre, for more than twenty years. My master, Yataro Okura, sent me off to Europe with these words: 'We Kyogen actors have been taught how to help the main actor in Noh, and to prepare the stage for them. When you go abroad, work in the spirit of trying to help your fellow actors instead of trying to draw the audience's attention to yourself. Disregard your own ego, and concentrate on creating a good environment for others to act in.'

With this final piece of advice, I left Japan.

1 Paris 1968 – The Start of the Centre International de Recherches Théâtrales

Paris 1968

I arrived in Paris. I had only known the city from pictures and films, and suddenly there it was, in front of my own eyes. It was the end of April. New leaves had just appeared on the branches of trees, and the buildings, the avenues, everything, were as beautiful as a dream. I could not conceal the grin on my face as I stood near the Louvre, looking up the Champs Elysées to the Arc de Triomphe. But this grin was accompanied by tears in my eyes. Tears caused by tear-gas that the police had thrown into a student demonstration. It was the beginning of the period of student unrest that contributed to the fall of President De Gaulle.

In the area round the Sorbonne, students dug up the cobble-stones and hurled them at the police. Even ordinary people and tourists were caught in the cross-fire, and there were some casualties. My hotel was situated in the middle of all this. I rarely managed the journey to a restaurant without tears running down my face.

Some Vietnamese students played an active part in the protests, and so people with oriental faces often attracted unwelcome police attention. I knew another Japanese actor who was chased up six flights of stairs by the police, and hit on the head with a stick. It took six weeks for him to recover. I tried to hide my face whenever I left the hotel. If I saw a policeman coming towards me, I would change direction and walk the other way. I had never wished so much that I had a European face. When I lived in Japan, I sometimes became self-conscious about my personal appearance, but never about my race.

In this part of Paris, after dark, I could hear the music of strip shows. As if nothing were happening round them, the girls continued to remove their clothes for the entertainment of visiting tourists.

And so, I began my work in Europe. I met Peter Brook for the first time in Jean-Louis Barrault's office at the Odéon Theatre. There were three Europeans: Brook, his assistant Geoffrey Reeves, and the brilliant Argentinian director Vittorio Garcia. I sat facing them, together with my interpreter. Brook, with his bright blue eyes, began.

An accident occurs in the middle of the street. A person, covered in blood, crawls out from a vehicle. Onlookers surround him. If that man suddenly stands up smiling, and bows to the onlookers, the onlookers are immediately transformed into an audience. And the man, covered in blood, becomes an actor. Without a stage, without lights, a theatrical situation has been created. At the same time, the difference between the real man and the fictional character, between reality and illusion, is more subtle here than in conventional theatre. I want to make some experiments to explore this principle. I would like to use actors from four countries; namely France, the USA, the UK, and Japan.

I thought that Brook was really quite extraordinary. I was used to working in the system where a play is chosen, the actors are given their parts which they learn, and then the whole thing is rehearsed to performance standard. Brook was proposing a completely new departure for me. I was also surprised to hear that he wanted to use a Japanese actor who spoke no French, alongside American and British actors. It would be as if the play were performed by deaf actors, and I could not see where all this would lead. But the translator told me that Brook was highly respected in Europe. He was seen as a forerunner of modern theatre, along with the Polish director Jerzy Grotowski, and Julian Beck of the 'Living Theatre'. This encouraged me to look forward to the start of rehearsals, though some fears about the unknown nature of the work persisted in my mind.

Our rehearsals took place at the Mobilier National, in the Gobelins district at the southern edge of Paris. It was a cold place, originally designed for the storage and exhibition of carpets and tapestries, and was surrounded by stone walls. I went there in my yukata, just as I would have done in Japan. I tried to behave like a 'proper Japanese actor'. But this Japanese actor felt rather small and shabby. All the actresses were my height or taller. And as for the men, they seemed like giants! Other members of the group included Glenda Jackson, Natasha Parry, Delphine Seyrig, and Michel Lonsdale. Surrounded by all these famous names, I stood in a corner feeling very small, regretting that I had come.

As we entered the working space, everyone was asked to close his or her eyes and discover the people nearby through touch. Then we were taken to another group to 'meet' them. As well as using our hands to make contact, we used our voices. We would make small 'ah' or 'oo' sounds as we touched each other. Eventually we became silent, and then on a signal, we all opened our eyes. There were about twenty-five of us sitting on the carpet together. It felt as if we had known each other for years, and yet we had only communicated through our hands and voices. This confirmed, through direct experience, that it was possible to communicate without words, and this surprised us all. This communication was not 'actor-to-actor' but 'human being-to-human being'. Later, I realised that this level of communication was central to theatre.

I used to think that in Western theatre the words of the text came first; that a script was necessary for a play. Each actor would learn to speak his or her lines very well, and then, because the text dictated it, they would exchange their lines in conversation with other actors. I thought that this presentation of the words of the text was what constituted 'Western theatre'. Now, I understand that theatrical expression is not simply a matter of sharing the speaking of text with another actor, but of discovering the underlying motivation which provokes their specific conversation. In a sense, the words of the text come second.

When two actors are really performing together (and not just saying lines at each other), the audience can sense that 'something' is happening between them. This 'something' is not emotion or psychology, but is more basic. For example, when you reach out and touch someone's hand it is a simple action. There may not be any story, or psychological reason, or emotion behind the gesture, but a genuine and fundamental exchange between two people has occurred. It is hard to find the words to describe exactly what has been exchanged. Perhaps we could call it 'physical sensation', or 'fundamental human energy'. Whatever we choose to call it, actors must engage in this process of exchange in order to create 'theatre'. No matter how cleverly you explain things through the words of the text, without this essential exchange, 'theatre' doesn't happen. Each actor must strive to find and hold this level of contact, and when it occurs, the whole text comes alive.

How much can we actually communicate to others through the use of words? If someone says 'I love you', can you really believe them? The phrase 'I love you' has been so over-used that it no longer carries meaning. It communicates nothing. For us to confirm the existence of love, we must have an insight, backed by experience. And words can be a hindrance in this respect.

9

Through that international meeting on the carpet, I discovered the pleasure of being a part of a larger unity. This is a deeply moving experience and something to be treasured. But this joy we find when we lose ourselves in a group or another person can be manipulated and twisted. Fascist movements exploit this pleasurable feeling and use it to propel people emotionally towards a chosen goal. This powerful sensation of group identity can be either positive or negative, depending on what creates it and how it is used. In theatre, we can use it positively to create company cohesion. Brook would say that a theatrical performance is like a game of football. Everybody must feel that they are members of a single team, working together.

That first exercise in Paris was a revelation to me, but gradually the emotional impact subsided, and we went on to another exercise. It was an improvisation. In all my theatrical career, I had never done an improvisation!

All Japanese traditional theatre (Noh and Kabuki) is based on the idea of 'kata'. A 'kata' is a fixed convention of performance which has been handed down by the teacher to the student, and which must be faithfully copied in every detail. Each role in a play has its particular 'kata' which prescribes every single movement, vocal intonation, costume detail, and nuance of interpretation. As a consequence, all performances are identical, and essentially unchanged from generation to generation. In this sense, the Japanese use of 'kata' resembles the Western system of classical music, or classical ballet.

Equally, in Japanese modern theatre twenty years ago, nobody used improvisation. Most directors still thought in terms of 'kata'. Even Shakespeare was performed in this way. A director would see a Shakespeare play in London, and would attempt to reproduce exactly what he had seen when he returned to Japan. There was no creative work involved, merely the imitation of external forms. Of course, in the twenty years since I left Japan, modern theatre there has changed considerably. But at that time it was still a question of copying Western actors and directors. Equally, there was no question of changing or developing a production during the performance run. After the first night, the production could never be changed and each moment had to be reproduced in exactly the same way every time. The performance had become 'traditional'.

Since all my theatrical training was based on 'kata', and even in modern theatre I had continued to work in the same way, an improvisation was a totally new experience. It was like jumping off a cliff. I had to gather enormous courage. I had absolutely no idea how to approach this kind of work. To crown it all, the themes themselves were strange.

At first you are water, then the water gradually gathers momentum and becomes a wave. Then it turns into a storm, and finally a typhoon. After this you become a human being who has been engulfed by the typhoon. You are totally exhausted, and just float on the surface of the water.

At first you are wind, and then the wind becomes stronger and transforms into fire. The fire rages, then eventually becomes soil.

The foreign actors were moving and twisting their bodies, crawling across the floor, and making loud sounds with their voices. If this pitiful little Japanese actor had tried to do the same thing, among all these tall, well-built people, it would have looked as if a mosquito were buzzing round the room. I, a Japanese man, would have made a fool of myself.

So I wondered what a 'proper Japanese actor' would do. The teachings of Noh came to mind. In Noh, everything is expressed in the 'hara'. The 'hara' is a point in the body, just below the navel. It is considered to be the centre of a person's energy and sense of being. As an actor, if you are really clear and determined in your 'hara', then your intention will be visible to

11

an audience, without needing a great deal of external elaboration. This emphasis on interior focus is true for all the arts. For instance, in Western music, a stream can be expressed through the use of a single drum, while the sound of great flood-waters requires five drums of varying sizes. To Westerners, a 'larger' sound requires louder instrumentation. However, in the music of Noh theatre, the same small hand-drum is employed to express the two different sounds of snow falling and the raging of the typhoon. Both sounds are equally loud and they have very similar 'tunes' on the drum. The difference is created through the inner focus of the drummer. In Noh theatre, it is the interior that changes, not the exterior.

Thinking about this, I decided that I wasn't obliged to express the themes of Brook's exercises through exterior action. If my interior became water or fire, then the outer form would shape itself. So this 'Japanese actor' sat on the floor, like Buddha, concentrating himself with all his energy, so that he might transform into fire or water. I remained sitting, while, all around, large foreign men leapt and twisted with great vigour. It must have looked quite odd; a small Japanese man in a cotton kimono, sitting in the middle of all this wild activity. After the improvisation, the foreign actors came up and praised 'the Japanese actor', saying there was 'Zen' in his work. 'The Japanese actor' gave a sigh of relief. So far so good.

Perhaps by describing my work as 'Zen', they were actually referring to the use of minimalism, which is typical of many Japanese arts. It can be seen in traditional brush and ink painting, where the artist uses the smallest number of brushstrokes necessary to convey the chosen image. In general, Japanese artists attempt to express the maximum truth through a minimum of means, and this approach certainly corresponds to the spirit of Zen. Although artists use minimalist techniques, they are also attempting to suggest a greater reality that lies beyond the visual image. For example, we look at a painting

12

which depicts a tiny fishing boat moving among waves in a river. This is the surface image. But the flowing river water suggests the vast, surging power of the sea. It also suggests the even greater flow of the universe itself, while the tiny fishing boat can be seen as a representation of our individual lives. Human beings have a tiny, fleeting existence, but at the same time are related to the whole universe. You cannot resist the flow of the universe, yet you are equally aware of your unique and separate existence within it.

When viewing a painting like this, the onlookers appreciate the work on a number of levels. They can admire the technical skill of the artist, enjoy the literal image of the fishing boat, and at the same time reflect on their relationship to the universe.

Traditional Japanese art attempts to eliminate anything that is inessential. It reduces expression to the minimum necessary for communication, and also aims to make its impact on an instinctive level. In terms of acting, this means simple, almost primitive ideas which have universal meaning. Uncluttered gestures, everyday relationships. And then these primitive ideas are refined and polished, and so become 'art'.

'Simple' does not mean 'ordinary'. A 'simple' action is not one that just feels 'natural'. If I ask someone to walk across the stage, they tend to walk in their normal, habitual manner, as they do in daily life. But our 'natural' daily habits are in fact extremely complex. One person may hold the left shoulder higher than the right. Another may move the right arm more strongly than the left. These are very complex movements. 'Simple' means basic and universal. All babies cry in more or less the same way. All cats, whether living in Europe, Africa or Japan, move in more or less the same way. So to find a 'simple' walk, one which is just step, step, step, without anything extra, is very difficult. You must get rid of your habits, even though they feel quite 'natural' to you.

From the audience's point of view, simple actions can have a

13

profound effect. In Japan, I witnessed a Noh actor's performance of the role of an old woman whose son has been killed by a Samurai warrior. She enters the scene in order to confront this Samurai. As the actor slowly walked along the wooden causeway that leads to the stage in the Noh theatre, he managed to portray, just through walking, all the feelings that were inside this old woman; her loneliness, her anger at the warrior, and her desire to give up life. It was an incredible performance, and afterwards I went backstage to ask the actor how he had prepared himself. I though perhaps he was using something like the Stanislavski system to find an emotional memory, or was using a particular idea. He said his thoughts were as follows: 'She is an old woman, so I must use shorter steps than normal. About 70 per cent of normal length. And I must stop at the first pine tree after my entrance. As I walk, this is all I think about.'

Yet from the audience I could feel everything. By keeping his actions very simple, and holding his mind strongly focused on his physical task, he created a 'space' for the audience's imagination to work. His simplicity and 'emptiness' permitted the onlookers to read whatever they wanted into his actions. If he had done too many movements, and then obscured them with the unnecessary details which come from personal habits, the audience would have noticed the actor himself, rather than responding to the character he was portraying. Consequently, they would have been unable to immerse themselves in the spirit of the character.

I saw a similarly powerful performance given by Irene Worth, who played the role of Jocasta in Peter Brook's 1968 production of *Oedipus* at the National Theatre in London. The moment of Jocasta's suicide was particulary moving. On the stage was a tall wooden pyramid, shaped like a sword-blade. To indicate the act of suicide, Jocasta stood behind the pyramid and slowly bent her knees. She descended until her head rested on the tip of the pyramid. At that point, she opened her eyes and mouth very wide to portray the instant of death. It was a wonderful moment.

I met her afterwards and asked her about it. She said that she found it very difficult to bend her knees and control her body so that she didn't wobble during the descent. All her concentration had to go into what her body was doing, and so she wasn't able to think about 'acting' anything at all. But it was an extraordinary moment.

And so the actor 'hones' his or her art. By 'honing' I mean 'to clarify', or 'refine'. To clean away, not embellish. Once you have achieved this level of control, then you can add details and habits to your body as part of the character you are portraying. But these are the character's personal habits, not the actor's.

The voice works in the same way. When you are born you have a very strong voice. Babies can cry extremely loudly all night long, without damaging their tiny throats. But as we grow up we accumulate a lot of 'dust' in our minds and our bodies. And so, when you are about twenty, you may find that your voice has become small or weak. This isn't natural. If you take a simple sound like 'Ah' and can find a way to say it with the freedom and openness you had as a child, then it becomes pure and capable of expressing many things.

So when we 'clarify' our bodies and voices, we achieve the first step in becoming actors. But this is not enough. Babies have clear, simple actions, but they are not actors. Onstage, babies and animals are very interesting to watch, but they cannot fully engage the audience on a deeper level. They lack the concentration that an actor must have. And this concentration is total. Not just the thoughts, but also the will, the emotions, and the whole self.

We began work on *The Tempest*, employing a variety of approaches. During rehearsals, everybody used improvisation to explore many aspects and themes of the play, not just their own role. For example, the whole cast was divided into pairs, and each pair improvised the initial meeting of Ferdinand and Miranda. Peter asked everyone to improvise that scene, so that he could see all the possibilities of the situation. And then he chose the best one. That is what defines a director with a good eye: the ability to make the right choice.

Peter works like a sculptor. He makes one beautifully shaped piece, maybe in the form of a cube. Then he makes another shaped like a sphere. He looks at these two pieces and decides where they need to be in relation to each other. Perhaps the sphere needs to be on top of the cube, or vice versa. When all of the pieces have been assembled together, like a collage, a sense of meaning and unity emerges. I get the impression, when we begin our work, that while Peter has a clear idea of the general direction of each show, he has not decided the exact final shape. Nonetheless, he knows how to investigate and uncover possibilities. This is his talent. At the beginning of rehearsals, he tells everyone, including designers, musicians etc., about his general idea. Everybody then starts their own creative work, and Peter observes what they do. If someone is straying too far from his basic direction, Peter brings them back, but if they are on the right path, he doesn't interfere. When I began working with Peter, he said very little to me, so I started to get worried. But an English actor reassured me, saying, 'Don't worry. If your work is bad, he'll certainly tell you!'

My role was Ariel, a spirit. It had no fixed form; sometimes I turned into a bird, sometimes into the substance of air itself. But the actors who were playing the various Lords worked in a different way. Geoffrey Reeves suggested the idea of the seven deadly sins. Each actor had to choose one of them and then shape his body to it. He made a kind of puppet of himself, and then the puppet started to move, and then to speak. In this case, the creation of character was approached from the outside. The shaping of the body determined the nature of the person. We used this idea in the performance, though not all of the time. Sometimes the actors would perform in a normal, naturalistic style, while at other moments they would use this broader stylised physicality which was reminiscent of Peking Opera or Kabuki.

Through various exercises, Peter began to investigate ways of exchanging theatrical culture between East and West. This strand of his work became very strong in subsequent years, but the improvisations we did during *The Tempest* were probably the beginning. An English actor called Robert Lloyd was playing Ferdinand in the play, and he and I did an exercise together. We stood back to back. Robert spoke his lines from the play, and at the same time, I said the exact same lines translated into Japanese. I spoke them in the style of the Noh theatre which uses archaic language and heightened intonation patterns. Hearing the sound of the Noh style of delivery, and feeling the way the sound was produced in my body, gave Robert a taste of a different way of transmitting theatrical energy. This was not directly used in performance, since Peter never asked anyone to imitate any particular style, but it gave Robert a direct experience of the Japanese approach.

Glenda Jackson was asked to portray the boat, passengers included. In order to prepare for this role, Peter sat her down on the floor, and started asking her questions. I can't be sure what sort of things he asked, since I hardly understood any English at the time, but the questions seemed to be directed at evoking physical sensations and subconscious states. The questions seemed to follow this pattern. 'You are in the water . . . floating . . . how do you feel?' He also used a lot of pure sounds, and breath noises. As she sat there with her eyes closed, Glenda began to take on the underlying physicality of the boat, and her breath appeared to change. It was not the kind of mime-style improvisation where the actor imitates the external appearance of the object through shaping the body and copying the movement patterns. Nor were the questions aimed at clarifying the personal history and psychological landscape of a particular character. Peter seemed to be evoking deeper, subconscious

17

perceptions of physical reality; what actually happens to us when we take on another kind of existence. We all did a similar exercise on how it felt to drown. These exercises were very difficult to do. It isn't easy to make a marriage between mental concepts and physical sensations.

Another exercise that particularly impressed me was one we did with Vittorio Garcia. He divided the actors into two groups, one active, one passive. The passive group represented the passengers from the boat, who were sleeping after their ship-wreck. The active group were Ariel's spirit assistants. The active group then tried to wake the others very gently, using touch and sound. They didn't try to act the part of 'spirits', they just tried to softly engage the passive group. Through this exercise, we explored subtle ways of making contact and responding to each other, as actors and as characters. In another similar exercise, the passive group was very sad, and their active partners had to find a way to make them happy through touch, or words, or whatever. To cheer up my partner (Glenda Jackson) I told her the story of what happened when I stopped in Copenhagen on my way to Paris. I had gone into the city to look around, and eventually I needed to go to the toilet. But I couldn't work out where to go, and since I could only speak Japanese, I got into a terrible muddle. I told her this silly story, in my appalling English. Eventually, she laughed, and this made me feel so happy.

During the improvisations, I found the work very strange. From the point of view of the work we are doing today, it all seems a bit crude and even comic. But it was the beginning of a process, and we were all taking the first hesitant steps into the unknown, learning from our mistakes.

Just after beginning these initial explorations, we were inter-rupted. The French equivalent of Equity went on strike in sympathy with the 'May Revolution', and this affected the French actors within the group. We all went to the Place de la

République for a rally. Students, trade unionists and Equity members set off on a march to the Opéra. When we joined the Equity members, I saw many familiar faces who I knew from the screen. But I felt a bit uncomfortable in that situation. I had been invited to Paris by the Odéon Theatre which was subsidised by the French Government, and now I found myself in an anti-Government rally, yelling 'Death to De Gaulle' together with everyone else, without actually knowing anything about the political situation. Since I wasn't truly able to mix with the crowd, I decided to follow them as an observer. As for my own future in France, I was filled with anxiety. What was going to happen?

Since we all wished to go on working, the foreign members of the group, along with Brook, requested an interview with one of the leaders of the student strike. Brook stated: 'We are not satisfied with the current theatre situation in the West. This is why our group, including actors from four different countries, has gathered together. We want to re-evaluate theatre. Since what we intend to do is within the spirit of your revolution, will you let us continue our activities during your strike?'

This meeting proved unproductive, and we could only wait until the end of the strike. In the meantime, students had occupied the Odéon Theatre. The director of the theatre, Jean-Louis Barrault, had opened the doors to the students, and the theatre had become the headquarters for the revolution. The Minister for Culture, André Malraux, dismissed Barrault over this action. Since our producer had been sacked, we found ourselves literally thrown out onto the streets.

We waited for the strike to come to an end, hoping that we would be able to start rehearsals again. Despite our optimism, it kept getting worse. The Metro stopped. There were huge piles of rubbish in the streets. The skirmishes between police and students became fiercer. I felt anxious, and asked one of the British actors, 'What shall we do if the strike gets worse?'

'If necessary, we'll drive to Belgium. It will only take a couple of hours.'

This answer impressed me a great deal. To a nation as insulated as Japan, it sounds terribly convenient to be able to travel to another country without having to cross the ocean. Two hours away, there is another country, existing peacefully, which has a different machinery for running the state, with no demonstrations or fights. You just step over the border, and there you are. They even speak the same language. The national borders of Europe seemed most peculiar to me, and at the same time, most practical. Just a line on the map to distinguish one country from another. In Japan, our sense of national identity comes from sharing one language, one culture, and one territory for hundreds of years.

In other parts of the world, such as Africa, invading powers drew lines on the earth to make national boundaries. These lines are often quite arbitrary. Two people might share the same history, the same language, the same religion, the same culture, but because a line has been drawn between them, we say that they have different nationalities. I found this very strange.

London 1968

The strike escalated day by day. In the end we decided to escape from Paris. The airport and the railway stations were already closed, and even the road to Belgium was impassable, since all the petrol stations had gone on strike. I don't know how it came about, but a small airline company lent us a hand. We took off from a military airport in France, and landed at an RAF base somewhere on the outskirts of London. In 1968, London was a flourishing, exciting city, famous for the mini-skirt and the Beatles. The first thing I did was to change my French francs into English currency. I did this on the recommendation of an

English colleague, who warned me that the French currency would become valueless very soon. I was surprised and disturbed by this strange possibility. Like most Japanese at that time, I had never travelled overseas, and had no direct experience of fluctuating currencies, or shifting exchange rates. In addition, the Japanese currency had always been very stable, and so I had never questioned its value. I had always assumed that a banknote carried a fixed and immutable value. Now this turned out to be an illusion as well. I looked at my banknotes with a fresh eye. They were just pieces of rather grubby paper, decorated with numbers. What a strange invention! And how peculiar we humans are to have created such a bizarre concept!

Brook's group convened once again. Peter said that it would be a great pity if we disbanded now, since we had managed to come together from all over the world. He said that he would get the money to pay us from the British Arts Council and the Royal Shakespeare Company, although it wouldn't be very much. He asked all of us to stay and continue rehearsing for our experimental show. He added that during this period, we would have to lodge with British actors in their homes.

After he had finished speaking, all hell broke loose. Everyone started to argue, and one American actor jumped up, saying, 'I gotta phone my agent in the States!' But in the end, we all agreed to stay. My host was Henry Wolf. He was a fairly small actor, about five feet tall, with a very elegant English wife, who was also an actress. They lived near King's Road, Chelsea, which at that time was the centre of fashionable London.

And we continued work on the play, a story based on Shakespeare's *Tempest*. We were going to perform it at the Roundhouse, a former Victorian train shed situated in North London. We were booked in for a week's performances.

There was a small T-shaped stage and a lot of scaffolding. The audience could sit wherever they liked, with the exception of one side of the 'T'. So we were performing in an arc of 270 degrees, as well as using floor, stage and scaffolding. The actors were in the space before the audience arrived, and would move and transform themselves into whatever the scene demanded. The actors were 'such stuff as dreams are made on'. They began as members of the audience, then through their actions they created the illusion we call 'theatre'. There were displays of hatred between brothers, love between men and women, endless desires for material possessions. At the end of the performance, the entire cast spoke the 'We are such stuff . . .' speech together, using free-form improvisation. Each actor could go in and out of the speech as he or she liked, and perform it with any vocal pattern. The story ended with a celebration which included the audience.

The lines I spoke were a mixture of Shakespearean text in English and Japanese. The obvious question is 'Why Japanese?' Since Ariel came from another world, we felt he could speak an 'unknown' language, and to an English audience Japanese was unusual and unfamiliar. English, French and Japanese were all spoken on the stage, creating a strange sort of symphony. Peter Brook complimented me, saying, 'You are the first Japanese actor to speak Shakespeare in English on a British stage.' This made me grin. The audience consisted of professionals from the Royal Shakespeare Company and the National Theatre. The performance never opened to the general public.

Because of the type of production it was, we never really knew which roles we would be playing in the actual performance, so everybody tried very hard in the early rehearsals. Yet when the parts were distributed nearer the opening, I could see a very clear drop in the level of enthusiasm among those who had been given minor roles. As for myself, I always remembered the parting advice of the master of Noh theatre: 'Don't perform for yourself, but in order to help others.'

I followed my master's instructions, and acted to help others. I didn't waste time worrying whether or not the role I had been

22

given was important, or if I looked good on stage. I know this sounds a bit moralistic, and as if I were advocating my personal attitude as a matter of theatre principle. In fact, all I was trying to do was to escape from the jealousy and envy which are an inevitable part of the actor's profession. By strictly following my master's advice, I hoped to free myself from such torments.

There is something that we could call a 'sickness of the spirit'. Western people sometimes use the word 'egotism' to describe this phenomenon. In acting terms it can lead a performer to think in the following ways: 'I want to be better than the others . . . I have learned a technique, and now I can demonstrate how much I have learned . . . I must be very visible onstage . . . The show really ought to be done this way.'

All of these represent a certain rigidity of consciousness. If all the actors in a production are working and thinking in this way, the stage soon becomes lifeless. Ideally, you should have no fixed ideas about your relations with other actors, or what you want to express, or how the show should go. You should remain open, flexible, and generous in your acting.

One day, while we were performing *The Tempest*, the stage-manager came to see me and said, 'A Japanese friend of mine is coming to see the show tonight. Would you like to meet him?'

'Of course.'

'Then we'll meet in a pub after the performance.'

That evening, I checked the audience before the show, and there were four Japanese already sitting there. Nowadays it is quite common to spot Japanese people in theatre audiences anywhere in the world, but in 1968 it was very unusual. Even in the streets they were extremely rare, since Japanese mass tourism had not begun. Given the rarity of this encounter, I was very concerned about making a good impression on my countrymen. The Japanese translation of Shakespeare that I was using for my lines was in an old-fashioned mode of speech, like Kabuki. It was a bit of a mouthful at times. Normally I assumed that nobody in the audience could understand Japanese, so I wasn't very careful with my delivery. But that night, knowing that there were Japanese in the audience, I was extra careful not to make any mistakes.

After the show I went to the pub where my compatriots were waiting. But as soon as we attempted to converse it became clear that they did not understand Japanese at all. They were third-generation emigrants who had been born and brought up in Canada. For me this was a tremendous shock. I had never even considered the possibility that there could be 'Japanese' in the world who were unable to speak Japanese. I had always assumed that anyone who appeared to be Japanese could speak the language.

This made me question What is Japanese? What was that image I had clung to for so long, 'The Japanese actor'? Suddenly, my certainties about what it meant to be Japanese were being eroded. I realised that there were 'Japanese' people who did not speak Japanese, who did not eat Japanese food, did not wear the kimono, did not bow, did not go to Shinto shrines to pray, had nothing to do with Buddhist temples, and did not live on the islands of Japan. I also realised that 'Japanese people' cannot be defined as 'people who speak Japanese', but rather that Japanese is simply a language that happens to be largely used by Japanese people. And it is not the wearing of the kimono or the polite bowing that makes a person 'Japanese'. A person may choose to bow, and that person may happen to be Japanese. That's all there is to it.

Some people have said that there is a uniquely 'Japanistic' part that exists within the totality of any individual Japanese person. If such a thing exists, this 'Japanistic' part would have to be rooted very deeply; deeper than the surface habits like wearing the kimono, or eating Japanese food, or even speaking the Japanese language. During the Second World War, some people used the phrase 'the Spirit of Japan' to describe this unique and elusive quality. However, if this 'unique' quality is so intangible, and difficult to locate, it is probably more true to say that it doesn't exist at all.

In art, if somebody strongly asserts his or her cultural background, and uses their traditional approach, it may be possible to communicate on an international level. But somehow I feel this isn't real 'international communication'. It is more likely to be mere exoticism. I played the role of Ariel wearing a kimono, using the Noh style of acting, and people said they found it very interesting. But I wasn't very happy about it. Maybe I was just being praised for the exoticism of my actions. If that were the case, my acting would only be a kind of cultural tourism, valued by Westerners for its foreignness. My performance would become a sort of exotic souvenir, like a 'Happi' coat, or the dolls that visitors bring back from Japan.

In a sense, the questions I was asking myself echoed a general trend. Around the time we were doing *The Tempest*, the theatre world in Europe was in ferment. Up until that period, the most important aim of a production was to deliver the literary sense of the script to the audience. But in the late sixties, there was a move away from the script as the sole theatrical vehicle. Instead there was an interest in exploring, through work with voice and body, the deeper psychological messages buried within the human being.

In many of these experiments, various oriental approaches were investigated, including traditional Japanese techniques. This took Japanese artists by surprise. Things they had been doing for centuries were suddenly being praised by the Western avant-garde. They were amazed at foreign admiration of their techniques and the arduous training involved. This created a strange illusion in the minds of many Japanese artists; they began to believe that their work was in the global forefront of modern art. They started to think that they were indeed 'modern artists'. In fact, it was mere coincidence that Western re-examination of European artistic concepts and techniques had led to approaches similar to those found in Japanese traditional arts. The work of traditional artists had become significant to modern experimentation by sheer accident.

Nonetheless, there were some artists in Japan who sought to apply traditional art in a modern way, and they have recently achieved international success. However, the desire to amalgamate traditional techniques and contemporary concerns has occasionally led to productions where Kabuki or Noh style acting has just been pasted on top of a modern script. There is nothing wrong with doing a modern production in Kabuki style, but the means of expression must be chosen according to the character of the piece. Not all scripts can be performed in Noh or Kabuki style, even if you explain that it is being done in accordance with Japanese tradition. If the audience cannot immediately grasp why the play has been done in that particular style because of the nature of the subject matter, it will only end up as a kind of empty exoticism, an exercise in style with no dramatic purpose.

A young Japanese actor once said to me, 'One day Japanese theatre will be the best in the world, in the same way that Japanese tape recorders and televisions became the best in the world, although at the outset, they were only imitations.' Japanese actors may feel flattered at this idea, but there is a confusion between technicality and creativity. Japanese industry may possess the latest technology in tape-recorder production, but it was not a Japanese inventor who had the crazy idea of putting sounds onto a ribbon of fabric. Japanese people are quite good at developing an idea and improving it technically. We are better at this than actually creating the initial concept. Personally, I have always felt the same about myself and my work.

I still wonder how I can be a 'true creative artist'. I suspect that the title refers to someone who possesses a traditional technique, who can understand the essence of traditional art, and yet is willing to explore and develop this in response to the modern world. If an artist only aims to acquire a technique, and does not attempt to find a contemporary meaning, then he or she cannot truly be called a 'creative artist'.

Our work on *The Tempest* came to an end. On my return to Japan, I decided that I wanted to investigate my own cultural tradition. My generation in Japan had been totally educated in a European way, without any reference to Japanese elements. For example, in music, we only learnt the Western system ('Doh, Re, Mi', etc.) and never studied traditional music. Similarly, in art we never discussed the work of Hokusai, only European theories of perspective, colour and composition. Even my own mental attitudes reflected Western patterns and approaches. Ironically, I had been studying traditional arts such as Noh since childhood. But while my body had learned Noh, and understood how to move in a Japanese way, my mind viewed the world of traditional theatre from a European perspective, like a tourist. I had no real understanding of the cultural and philosophical concepts that underlay Japanese tradition and art. So, not only was I divided between East and West, my body and my mind were in opposite camps! I decided it was time to learn something about my own tradition of philosophy and culture.

2 The Work Continues

The moment I got back to Japan, I started looking for ways to put my decision into action. I felt that Zen Buddhism was a good place to begin learning about my cultural heritage, and within a few days of returning to Tokyo, I had managed to arrange a visit to a temple. Those of us that had been abroad, even for a short period, were forced to confront our lack of real understanding of Zen. Living in Japan, we tend to assume that we know all about it, yet in fact we know nothing. I had read books but never actually sat in meditation. It was time to start doing it properly.

I went to a Zen training temple in Saitama. The students stayed there for three years of compulsory study, after which they would be officially qualified as priests. I was allowed to join by special arrangement. I was not permitted to enter the Za-Zen Dojo where the main meditation practice took place, but I was allowed to work in the kitchen, and to join the priests in the evening when everybody meditated together. This particular temple was part of the Rinzai sect, who often use 'koans' (paradoxical questions) to stimulate the student into greater awareness and spiritual understanding. Since I visited the temple outside the main period of meditation (called Dai-Sesshin), I was not given a koan to work on. This was a very relaxed period, just after the New Year. In this holiday atmosphere, one of the trainees (who are called 'Wansui') chatted about the three years of training, which involve complete celibacy. As part of the training, the Wansuis are obliged to wander through the countryside, begging for rice. While doing this, they wear traditional robes and a large straw hat that covers most of their face. The priest who was telling me about his experiences, said that as the Wansui goes from door to door, he peeps out from under his hat and sees various women, all of whom look wonderful. After three years without sex, all women seem beautiful to a Wansui. And this has led to the saying that 'Wansuis have adulterous eyes.'

The Head Priest of the temple was called Keizan Hakusui. Most priests leave their ordinary lives behind them and formally enter a temple between the ages of ten and fifteen. (This official renouncing of the world is called Shukke, and it is at this point that the head is shaved.) This particular old master had done Shukke at the age of twenty-one, so people teased him by calling him a 'late-shaver priest'. I only had the honour of meeting him once, but when he discovered that I was an actor, he gave me a lot of excellent advice. 'When you hold up a tea-bowl,' he said, 'hold it as if it weighs hundreds of pounds. When you lift up a small table, it should seem like a huge mountain.'

He was not referring to 'miming' the heaviness of the tea-bowl, but of giving the gesture the full 'weight' of concentration. In this way, the action becomes 'simple' and 'empty'. Uncluttered, uncomplicated, yet full of meaning for the audience. The priest went on to say: 'In Za-zen [sitting meditation], there are three important things: the energy in the Tan Den [a point in the lower abdomen], "Kufu" ["Exploring the paths"], and "San-mai" ["Self-immersion"]. As you work towards understanding of "Mu" ["Nothingness"], it is not an empty "Nothingness" that you pursue. It has to be "Mu" imbued with force and energy. In Za-zen you have to keep your lower abdomen firm, since the Tan Den is the centre of the body's energy. You cannot reach the state of "Nothingness" without rigorous self-examination.

29

You have to explore many paths within yourself. That is "Kufu". Once you are in the state of "Mu", you simply concentrate. Do nothing. Nothing at all. Immerse yourself deeply in it. That is "San-mai". These are the ways of Zen. And these same ways can be applied in the theatre.'

I had already realised the importance of clarity and 'emptiness' as a theatrical goal. He had now given me three paths that would help me reach that goal. Japanese actors have been told for centuries to concentrate their force in the lower abdomen. This is the first step. And in order to fully grasp a role, an actor has to explore many different ways ('Kufu'). Finally, when you are performing, you cannot disperse your attention; you need to concentrate fully on your role ('San-mai'). Ultimately, to perform well is more or less the same as doing Zen. The first great master of Noh theatre, Motokiyo Zeami (who lived and wrote about theatre in the late fourteenth and early fifteenth centuries) made a similar point. 'When you are concentrating well, you enter a state where you feel as if you are flying.' This inner state must be the same as that experienced in Zen. It means you are no longer in your ordinary world of time and space; instead you have entered a different realm.

At the beginning of 1970, I received a letter from Peter Brook, saying:

> I am planning to start the 'Centre International de Recherches Théâtrales' (International Centre for Theatre Research). It will last for three years. The members will be theatre people: directors, writers, musicians, artists and actors from all over the world. It will question the fundamentals of theatre, such as: 'What is Theatre?', 'What is an Actor?', 'What is an Audience?' These questions will be examined from the very beginning without any preconceptions. It will be based in Paris. Would you be interested in participating?

My original aim when I started working in theatre was to become a director, and eventually form my own company. I had already been working in films and television for some years, but I didn't feel that this really equipped me for the stage. I also believed that a good director needs more than a theoretical understanding of theatre; it is equally necessary to learn concrete techniques. To acquire these skills, I had joined a theatre company in Tokyo called the Bungaku-za, and I made a firm decision to stay with them for ten years, thinking, 'After ten years, when I become an actor worthy of the name, I will leave and set up my own company and work as a director.' This was the promise I made to myself.

Unfortunately, I discovered that I wasn't getting anywhere at the end of the ten years with Bungaku-za. There didn't seem to be a single special talent in me, least of all the one necessary for the job of director. As time went on, I felt a sense of gnawing disappointment with myself. I was in this state of mind when I went to Europe and met Peter Brook. In him I felt I had actually encountered a true director. After my return to Japan, my sense of personal disappointment continued and intensified. When the second invitation arrived, it seemed like a helping hand stretched towards me, at a time when I had lost all hope. And so I thought: 'I'll go and learn stage directing at Brook's centre. It means that I'll have to continue acting for a while, but I want to learn Brook's approach to theatre, and to see how he works. Yes, I'll take this job. However, three years seems rather a long time. After three years' absence, I might not be able to find work back in Japan. It might even mean that I have to abandon my own country.'

I decided to take the risk of leaving Japan, but I never imagined that those three years were the beginning of twenty years of drifting round the world.

At that time in Japan, the student demonstrations against the Japanese–American Treaty (which agreed a continuing US military presence on Japanese soil) had ended without gaining much popular support or recognition. The Government had started to exert firmer control over the students through the use of a stronger police force. This phenomenon was also occurring in the West. In many countries, governments were becoming more right wing, using police or military power. The kind of demonstrations seen in the Paris revolution or the anti-Vietnam War movements became almost unthinkable.

Just as I was preparing to leave once again for Europe, a friend gave me a book to read on the plane. It was the *Book of Tea* by Tenshin Okakura. About a hundred years ago, Okakura had left Japan to visit Europe, where he eventually died. He wrote the book to show Europeans that Japan had a culture of its own, and was not simply a distant, barbaric country. The Tea Ceremony is an important part of Japanese culture and philosophy. A full Tea Ceremony requires a specially built tea 'room': a small building made from simple materials, often overlooking a garden. Once the date of the ceremony has been agreed, the Tea Ceremony master prepares for his invited guests. He chooses beautiful, yet unostentatious tea-bowls, boils the water in a special kettle, and arranges the space to create an atmosphere of tranquil harmony. The guests enter, sit, and then watch the master prepare the tea using an established series of ritual movements. As they drink the tea, the guests may quietly discuss the beauty of the tea-bowls or some similar topic. At the end of the ceremony they bow, thank each other, and then depart back into the real world, refreshed and having gained a sense of calm openness. This is the purpose of the Tea Ceremony. Through a simple everyday action, harmoniously performed, the spirit of the participants is renewed.

I began to read the book on the flight to London. It touched me deeply, yet I cannot really explain why. Probably the writer was a man living far away from home, and because he was missing his country, he had an urge to idealise it, and so produced this book. There I was, sitting in an aeroplane, leaving Japan on my own, and having no idea what fate had in store for me. I recognised my own feeling of insecurity as I read this book, and the recognition eased my tension a little. The following extract seemed particularly interesting:

The long isolation of Japan from the rest of the world, which was so conducive to introspection, has been highly favourable for the development of the Way of Tea. Our home and habits, costume and cuisine, porcelain, lacquer, painting – our very literature, have all been subject to this influence.

As I mentioned earlier, Japan had isolated itself from outside influence for many centuries. In the absence of fresh stimuli arriving from overseas, Japanese culture had tended to develop through the constant refinement of already existing forms. This led to a focus on detail and nuance, and this focus was extended to all areas of daily life. It can be seen today in the way Japanese food is prepared and meticulously presented. In the same way, the Tea Ceremony was an artistic refinement of an everyday action.

The Tea Ceremony is also linked to Zen Buddhism. It is one of the 'Ways' of achieving spiritual awareness and understanding. Many of the comments Okakura makes in his book refer to this dimension of the ceremony. For example:

Those who cannot feel the littleness of great things within themselves, are apt to overlook the greatness of little things in others.

There is no single recipe for making the perfect tea, as there are no rules for producing a Titian, or a Cézanne.

The reality of a room, for instance, is to be found in the vacant space enclosed by the roof and walls, not in the roof and walls themselves. The usefulness of a water pitcher dwells in the emptiness where water might be put, not in the form of the pitcher, or the material of which it was made. The vacuum is all-potent because it is all-containing. Only in a void does motion become possible. Anyone who could make himself a vacuum into which others can freely enter, would become a master of all situations. The whole can always dominate the part.

The next quote also interested me, since it seems as relevant today as it was a hundred years ago.

It is greatly to be regretted that so much of the apparent enthusiasm for the Art of Tea at the present time has no foundation in real feeling . . . In this democratic age of ours, men clamour for what is popularly considered to be the best, regardless of their true feelings. They want what is costly, not what is refined; what is fashionable, not what is beautiful . . . The name of the artist is more important to them than the quality of the work.

Back in England again, I went to Stratford-upon-Avon, where I spent a month watching rehearsals of *A Midsummer Night's Dream*, directed by Peter Brook. Since I had come to Europe to study directing, I wanted to observe Brook's working methods before going into research with him. As I was watching one rehearsal, Brook explained his approach in the following way.

If during a scene, a director asked an actor to perform while walking on the ceiling, the actor would think that the director was completely mad and refuse to even consider the idea. Therefore, I don't suggest anything to the actor, I just say 'Play it as you like'. In most cases, the actor would choose to utter the line while sitting on a chair. But if I had

34

arranged things so that the chair broke when he sat on it, he might decide to speak while wandering about on the stage. But if the stage was covered in oil and then set alight, the actor would be forced to perform on a table. Again, if the table had been designed to break, the actor would realise that he could not use the chair, the floor, or the table. In desperation he would turn to the director for help. When this happened, the director would not need to say a single word. Just pointing to the ceiling would suffice. And the actor would think, 'Of course! The ceiling! What a brilliant idea!' And willingly try to find a way to do it.

During the rehearsal period, I invited a few people, including Brook and his wife Natasha Parry, back to my flat for a Chinese meal. As I wasn't a very good cook, I decided to simply fry some meat and vegetables together in a pan. While I was clumsily chopping various bits and pieces, Brook watched me, and then said:

Directing has something in common with cookery. The cook prepares for the meal by assembling the various ingredients before the guests appear, and once they have arrived, he tosses everything into the pan. The taste is not created by the cook himself, but occurs as the ingredients mix together in the hot oil. Combining together all the diverse elements creates the special flavour. As far as the cook is concerned, the taste is at the mercy of God. However carefully he has prepared, if the ingredients are incompatible with each other, there is nothing he can do. Directing is exactly like that. The actual flavour is made by the actors working together. The director's task is merely to prepare as much as he can for the actors, so that they can create a marvellous dish. Once the audience is in the theatre and the curtain is up, everything depends on the actors. Therefore, the most important task for a director is to prepare well.

The rehearsals for the *Dream* involved some fascinating exercises. One event that particularly interested me was an open rehearsal for an audience of children. Before beginning the rehearsal, Brook said to the company:

No matter how profound a piece is on an artistic or philosophical level, if the underlying story is not understood by the audience, it cannot be called a play. Let us try tonight, in front of a young audience, to see how much we can make them understand, while putting aside all our complex theories about the deeper meaning of the play.

Afterwards, he said to me: 'In Shakespeare's time, the audience contained royalty, aristocrats, intellectuals, labourers and children. All the classes enjoyed the theatre together. Nowadays, audiences are divided into "Commercial Theatre Goers", "Fringe Theatre Goers", and "Classical Theatre Goers". Despite the difficult conditions today, I would like to develop a kind of theatre that could be enjoyed by everyone, just as it was in Shakespeare's time.'

Paris 1970

We moved back to Paris in November 1970 and started our auditions for the Centre International de Recherches Théâtrales. There were already about ten actors, including myself, who had been selected previously for the research work. Other people had come from all over the world wanting to join us, and naturally we wished to give them the opportunity of participating. We also wanted to see how they worked. For about a month, Brook ran improvisations in groups of five or six, in order to find talented actors.

Working as Brook's assistant, I led improvisations with actors from all over the world. I was now able to do improvisations

36

easily and freely, and could afford to spend time observing what I thought might be national characteristics. I noted down my initial impressions.

USA: Hard workers, and the body moves well. Also speak lines fluently. Are good at being realistic, but as actors, they find it difficult to relate to systems of stylisation, abstraction, or metaphysical transfer. In Zen painting and Noh theatre, the performance is the result of rigorous selection and severe cutting-back. Their approach is the opposite of this. They are good at laughing, and frank as friends. Nice people to be with.

French: Intellectually very sharp. Display brilliant ideas in improvisation, but they sometimes perform as if they existed only as a brain, while their bodies have no reality. Usually late for rehearsal.

African: Movement is beautiful and the voice is excellent. It is clear that they have something wonderful, but it seems that what they present is their own 'self', not something they have created through acting. Their way of thinking is complex, and it is sometimes difficult to know what is happening inside.

English: Their acting appears the best among the Europeans. Intelligence and body are well balanced, and their ability to give form to a concept or an idea is excellent. Creativity is good, and they are never late for rehearsal.

These were very superficial impressions written when I first arrived in Europe. I now realise that these images are far too simplistic, and do not reflect the complexity of each culture, nor the variety of performers in each region.

Through these improvisations, Brook selected his actors. A long time afterwards, during a symposium, Peter was asked, 'What kind of actors do you look for?' He replied, 'The kind of actor who can open himself, and freely communicate with others. The one who can express more than the director's imagination.'

But I sometimes think that he tends to prefer problematic

actors; actors who would not be too easily convinced by Brook; the ones who ardently defend their own ideas; the ones who can't always see what Peter is getting at. Actors like myself, who are obedient, and say 'Yes' to everything, are too tame for him. On a certain level, Peter likes to have a hard time with actors. Since his actors are free to say whatever they think, and Peter is always ready to listen, there is a lot of interesting communication.

Back in 1968, we continued our improvisations until the membership of the CIRT was complete. Americans, Europeans, Africans, Middle Easterns and Far Easterns were gathered together, and it seemed a 'mini-global community'. The French Government gave us a hall in the Mobilier National, which had been built to display giant Gobelin tapestries, to use as a studio. The researchers/actors were all paid a monthly salary. As the work of the CIRT developed, the number of researchers varied – sometimes around fifty, sometimes as few as ten.

This mini-global community became to some extent a real community, even outside our theatre research activities. We did not live together, but the work on acting was directly connected to our real lives, and real life affected our research. This was inescapable. The principle behind Brook's work was that those of the group who came from a different genre or tradition of theatre would open up and share their knowledge with the others. Through this process of mutual exchange, we sought a new gateway to a new theatre, and at the same time, a new relationship between the individual and the group. For this we had to question the very structure of theatre.

It was not so much that our work together in the studio created a sense of community, but rather, when our community gathered in the empty space, and someone started to tell a story, then the space began to function as a theatre. Our sense of community was not pursued as an end in itself. It was a necessary part of our work as actors involved in creating and exploring theatre.

38

There is another important point about the group's work: no one must insist on their personal point of view. Everyone must be free to react to whatever happens within the space. Then they can discover something completely new. As Peter often says, 'Be open, be free. Don't be disturbed by anything.'

Of course, this sort of freedom is very difficult to achieve in practice. Your concentration must not be locked into any one idea or situation. It must be free to go anywhere. If you rigidly fix your concentration in one specific place, all the other possibilities become empty and lifeless. Keep your concentration wide and fluid. Then you can be truly open.

This idea was illustrated by one of the first exercises we did with Brook. We visited the zoo. In fact, we went there often, and when we came back, we spent a lot of time discussing what we had seen. (Observing animals was a very good exercise for an international group which had no common language. Although we couldn't speak to each other, we could easily communicate as animals!) Brook said: 'Animals move beautifully because they have no tension in their bodies. But they are not totally relaxed either. They are always ready to move at any moment, in order to escape attack, or to pounce on their prey. Animals maintain two physical states at the same time. The body is free and well balanced, and the mind is focused and aware. Consequently, the animals can react quickly. They can leap in any direction, they can use their strength, or they can employ delicate precision. This must be the fundamental state of the actor onstage. It is very important to observe this today, since there is a great deal of misunderstanding about what "relaxation" really means.'

Both body and mind need to be 'awake' and 'ready', but this does not involve any kind of rigidity or tension.

Imagine you are being attacked by ten people at the same time. If you fix your concentration on only one of these attackers, you will be killed by the other nine. However, if you focus on responding to each attack as it happens, irrespective of who is delivering the blow, then you can react effectively. Your mind is constantly floating in the moment. You don't think about the attack that has just occurred, or what might come next. Just respond, and then immediately move on to the next attack. It will seem that you are only fighting one person. If you think about your ten adversaries, you will be overwhelmed. But if you fight in the moment, it is only one attack. On the stage it is similar. Just remain open to the other actors. Don't fix your attention on any one aspect of the performance. Allow yourself to respond to your fellow performers, and then you will discover how your character reacts.

However, reacting to other actors is only half of the process. You must also maintain your own purpose. For example, you are painting a self-portrait. Your aim is to create an accurate likeness, and you are concentrating on this task. But people keep coming up to you to ask questions, and you have to give them an answer immediately. Someone else stealthily approaches you, and you must judge whether or not they mean harm. You hear music coming from somewhere, and you enjoy listening to it, or even join in the singing. You react fully to everything in the outside situation, but still keep concentrated on your own task. As an actor your concentration is not focused on simply reacting to outside events, or on sustaining your own role. Your attention should be focused on both areas simultaneously.

When I left Japan for the second time, Yataro Okura, my Kyogen teacher, gave me some more advice. He counselled me to acquire something called 'Ri-ken no Ken'. This is a phrase used in the writings of Zeami, the founder of Noh theatre. 'Ri-ken' literally means 'outside view'. It is the opposite of 'Ga-ken', meaning the performer's own subjective view of himself and his actions. To have 'Ri-ken no Ken' means that the actor is able to see his performance from the outside, as if through the eyes of the audience, and can accommodate his work to their perceptions.

Acquiring this 'Ri-ken no-Ken' proved an interesting task. Initially, when performing or doing improvisations, all my attention was taken up with watching my partner and working out what to do next. There was no time for 'Ri-ken no Ken'. But as time passed I gradually understood what he meant. Several years afterwards, I met Okura again, and said to him:

'I originally thought that the 'Ri-ken no Ken' viewpoint was physically located in the audience; that it meant watching myself from the auditorium. But now I realise that this viewpoint is situated behind me. I watch myself acting from somewhere behind my head.'

Okura smiled and said, 'Yes, that's right. Your true self watches you from behind.'

When he said that, I felt very pleased with myself.

This freedom of concentration is very difficult for beginners. If an untrained person tries to work without any fixed point of concentration, they usually end up with no concentration at all, rather than a free and fluid awareness. You must train the concentration, just as you train the body. In Japanese classical theatre we begin this training by asking the student to focus their concentration on the 'hara', the point, about three centimetres below the navel, which is considered to be a major energy centre. Young actors are asked to stay aware of this area at all times, and to use it as the starting point for all their actions. Sometimes people make the mistake of assuming that keeping your concentration on your 'hara' is the ultimate aim, but in fact it is only the first stage in learning about concentration. Once you have understood how to focus your concentration with your body, as well as your mind, then you learn to release it and let it travel freely. In a sense, once you have learned the technique of total concentration, then you forget about it. Ultimately, you should never have to concentrate on concentration. You should have no consciousness of what your consciousness is doing.

This raises the question of how to train an actor. In traditional Japanese theatre, which uses fixed forms of expression, the physical and vocal techniques are clearly prescribed. You copy exactly what your teacher does. There is no improvisation or personal expression. When you start to learn these techniques, you have to concentrate very hard on what you are doing, how to move, how to balance, how to reproduce your teacher's actions exactly. But when you have gone very far into the training, you don't have to think about how to do the actions any more. They have become natural, and so your consciousness becomes freer. The aim of all systems of technical training is to enable you to do an action without worrying about how you do it. But unless you have this training you cannot arrive at this freedom of communication.

In modern theatre, where the actor is required to be creative, it is more difficult. I feel that there is still a need for technical training in order to free the body from its daily habits, and to establish control of the consciousness. Once these have been learnt, they can be thrown away. In a sense, the technical training of an actor is not directly used when working in the theatre. It is merely a part of the process of learning how to act with freedom. You train in order to acquire a technique, which you then throw away, in order to perform creatively.

There is one danger with technical training. You may become a prisoner of the technique. I often see someone moving on the stage, and it is evident that they have had classical ballet training. There is nothing wrong with doing classical ballet as part of an actor's training, but it should not be visible in their performance (unless this is specifically intended). You undertake technical training in order to eliminate your personal habits and make your actions clear and 'simple'. You should not simply replace personal patterns with technical patterns. When this happens, the actor has become a prisoner of the training system.

Similarly, when I run workshops, people often ask me, 'How can I use this exercise in a performance?' That is the wrong question. Students need to discover their own ways of acting. But I made the same mistake when I was young. I learned a lot of different techniques and was always thinking about how to use them in the theatre. Over the years, as I worked with Brook, I had to throw away all my carefully learned techniques. Eventually I discovered that the only thing you really need is freedom.

3 Remembering Japan

The work of the CIRT commenced, and, as Peter had indicated in his letter of invitation, it aimed to re-examine the very roots of theatrical communication. In his book, *The Shifting Point*, Peter describes the objectives and practice of the CIRT in the following way:

Together, we confronted the difficulties of theatre in its present form and felt the need to re-explore it through a new structure. We wanted to get away from the idea of a company and yet we did not want to shut ourselves away from the world, in a laboratory . . . We felt that research in the theatre needs to be constantly put to the test in performance and performing, and needs all the time to be refreshed by research with the time and conditions it demands – and which a professional company can seldom afford . . . The centre was also a point where different cultures could converge: the centre was also a nomad, taking its mixed group on long journeys to interact with people never touched by a normal theatrical tour. Our first principle, we decided, was to make culture, in the sense of culture that turns milk into yoghurt – we aimed to create a nucleus of actors who could later bring ferment into any wider group with whom they worked. In this way, we hoped that the special privileged conditions we were making for a small number of people could eventually enter into the theatre's mainstream . . . So, of course, everyone asks, 'What exactly do you do?' We call what we are doing 'research'. We are trying to discover something, to discover it through what we can make, for other people to take part in. It demands a long, long preparation of the instrument that we are. The question always is: are we good instruments? For that we have to know: what is the instrument for? The purpose is to be instruments that transmit truths which otherwise would remain out of sight. These truths can appear from sources deep inside ourselves or far outside ourselves. Any preparation we do is only a part of the complete preparation. The body must be ready and sensitive, but that isn't all. The voice has to be open and free. The emotions have to be open and free. The intelligence has to be quick. All of these have to be prepared. There are crude vibrations that can come through very easily and fine ones that come through only with difficulty. In each case the life we are looking for means breaking open a series of habits. A habit of speaking: maybe a habit made by an entire language. A mixture of people with lots of habits and without even a common language have come together to work.

One of the major themes in our first year's research was the use of voice and language. We started by examining how actors communicate when they cannot understand each other's language. Our first exercise involved throwing various swear-words at each other: 'Aho' (fool), 'Baka' (stupid), 'Otanko-Nasu' (small aubergine), 'Cunt', 'Mother-fucker', 'Cock-sucker', 'Putain' (whore), 'Con' (vagina). It seems that Japanese swear-words (the first three noted above) are very moderate compared to those of some other countries! We experimented with these words as pure sounds, while forgetting about their meaning. It seems that they are powerful, not just because of the meaning of the words, but also through the energy of their sound. When you pronounce those sounds you feel as if you are attacking someone. In all languages this is the case. Powerful swear-words have strong sounds. Probably these words became popular as a way of attacking others because they were pleasurable to speak. Each sound has its own particular energy. The feeling inside you when you say 'Ah' is different to when you say 'Ee'. If you put a strong sound with a strong physical action, then that action is easier to do. Using the sound gives you more energy than doing it in silence. The sounds themselves seem to carry specific connotations. For example, I pronounce two Japanese words, 'Ikuru' (ee-kee-roo) and 'Shinu' (shee-noo). The first means 'life', and the second 'death'. When I ask the listener to say which is which, in almost every case, even those who cannot speak Japanese select 'ikiru' to mean 'life'. It would seem that the sounds alone create a sense of meaning.

Similarly, Brook pointed out that when you perform Shakespeare, the play itself has its own energy. Any written play's energy comes from the combination of meaning and sound. Since Shakespeare is an extraordinary writer, his plays have an enormously strong energy. People sometimes try to perform Shakespeare in a normal naturalistic way. They study the text, make certain decisions about the character, clarify what he feels at a particular point in the play, and then speak the appropriate lines with that emotion. They say 'Hamlet is feeling sad when he says "To be or not to be . . .",' and then they speak those lines in a sad way. If you do this, you are not entering the world of Shakespeare, you are bringing Shakespeare down into your world, down to the level of your own personal experience. This is a considerable loss, since Shakespeare's realm of possiblities is vaster than any single person's experience of life. It is interesting to try working another way. In the beginning, make no decisions about the text, just say the words out loud. As you listen to the sound of the text and observe how the words shape your tongue and lips, then you may find that certain feelings are evoked. Through these physical sensations you start to enter Shakespeare's world, and you can make new discoveries about the character. Of course, it is not enough to say the words out loud. You must listen and be responsive to what is happening inside you. Try to go into the text through its sound.

Many years later, when we were performing *The Mahabharata*, we did it first in French and later in English. Before we started work on the English version, we did an exercise to give the actors the sensation of how it felt to use the English language. An English actor chose several famous phrases from Shakespeare. He spoke them and then we copied his exact words and style of delivery. At a certain moment, despite not being able to understand the meaning of the words, I was touched very deeply by the sounds I was pronouncing. I felt I was tasting something of Shakespeare's world.

Back in the first year of the CIRT's work, this research on sound and feeling led to a certain amount of confusion. People, hearing rumours about our explorations, began to believe that Peter was leading us to abandon thought and meaning, in order to plunge into an underworld of emotion. In fact, the research had a quite different aim. The intellectual content of a text is studied everywhere: our task was to concentrate on the aspect of language that had become sadly neglected over the centuries: the vibratory power of its sound.

As a next step, we created our own dialect. We took words from various languages and jumbled them up together to create interesting sounds, e.g. 'Bashta hondo stofklock madai zutto'. We had to create a meaning for this phrase according to the situation that was being improvised. Working with a partner (who obviously didn't know the literal sense of your words), you had to communicate what you wanted to say through your use of intonations and clarity of intention. We worked a great deal in this created language, which eventually became known as 'Bashtahondo'.

We also discovered that communication is possible through body movement. However, the first thing you need for this is an articulate body. To help us develop this, Brook gave each of us three bamboo poles. The first was one metre in length, the second, one and a half metres, and the third, two metres long.

We used the sticks for three purposes. Firstly, we used them as a way of 'measuring' the body, and becoming aware of basic positions. For example, you hold the stick vertically. Is your body absolutely parallel to the stick? Or is it at another angle? With the stick you can see your positions very clearly. In daily life you never consider whether your hand is absolutely vertical, or at 45 degrees, but the sticks made us aware of these details. Then we started to use the sticks as extensions of the body. If you hold the end of the stick in your hand, it makes your arm very long, and any gesture you make with that arm will be amplified. This made us very aware of our actions, where we placed them, and what they represented as 'signs'. Even the tiniest gesture became visible, since it was being enlarged by the stick. You had to be aware of each movement, and be clear about what that gesture conveyed to the onlooker. The third way we used the sticks was in terms of relationships. We could hold them, throw them away, balance them on our heads. Finally, we made some sequences of movements using the sticks. For example, everybody stood in a circle holding one end of their own stick in both hands. The other end of the stick touched the ground in front of the person. Everybody slowly raised the tip of their stick, lifting it until the pole was completely vertical. There was no leader for this exercise; it was done in silent unison. We did this exercise two years later in front of an audience in an African village, during our journey across the Sahara (described in Chapter 5).

Until we began this exercise, the people watching us were very bored and restless, shifting about and chatting with their neighbours. But when the exercise commenced, they suddenly stopped gossiping and became involved in what we were doing. The unity of the actors was clearly expressed through the use of the sticks, and this communicated itself to the audience.

In order to test our ideas on communication via body movement, we visited a school for deaf children. Their ages ranged between six and twelve. We performed stories using only movement, and sometimes did improvisations together with the children. Since the actors came from various countries, the communication within our own group was not vastly different to that which we experienced in the school. Personally, I found communication with deaf children easier than chatting with normal French children, since I couldn't speak or understand the language in any case! Although the children were good at picking up the images we created, they seemed to have more difficulty putting things together into a logical sequence. They often watched television programmes, but they received them without following the storyline. They tended to focus on the feelings visible in each scene and created their own explanations. As a result, it always ended up as a kind of fantasy. It was not easy to get those children to understand the storyline of our improvisations, or to follow directions.

While working at the school, we made another useful discovery. The truth of the relationship between the actors is as important as the text. In Japanese, we have two different words for the verb 'to see'. The first, 'ken', means to look at the outside, while the other, 'kan', means to perceive the interior. When you are having a conversation with a friend, you often just chat on the surface; your two 'outsides' are conversing. At other times, you are actively trying to discover what truth lies behind your friend's words; you are trying to see 'inside'. This is normal in daily life, but as actors we sometimes forget about it. We learn our text, and then listen to the other actors simply in order to pick up our cue for the next line. We don't have any real contact. Ideally, each character should be trying to look deep 'inside' the other characters in an attempt to understand what is happening. Characters within a play do not know what will happen in the following scene. They need to look 'inside' each other in order to work out what is going on, and what to do next. This is slightly different to the need for actors to be open with each other. This is the life of the characters themselves.

One day Brook gave me a task: 'As you want to be a director, here is something that might help you. Would you like to lead an exercise using the bamboo poles? What it involves is creating movements for the other actors. The group will form a circle, and will copy whatever you suggest. If you, as a leader, continue to give movements that are repetitive, the actors will soon get bored. So you will have to keep on changing what you do. For example, altering the pace from fast to slow. This goes for directing as well. In order to avoid boring the audience, you will have to vary the pace of the performance, using all available means. You should get the knack of it, through leading the exercise.'

On and off since then, I have continued to lead the exercise sessions which are held for the cast, prior to each show. It is compulsory to have an hour's warm-up. When leading these sessions, I focus on the following two areas. Firstly, to create a team spirit for the show. As Brook often says, the play cannot be created by a number of individual pieces of acting. It has to be created by a team working together. Therefore, exercises to unite the group are very important. Secondly, we need to cut off from the flow of ordinary daily life, to separate from the way we have lived prior to arriving at the theatre. We need to focus ourselves in a theatrical way. I believe that these two aims can be best achieved through vocal and physical exercises, not through theoretical discussions. We do a lot of work standing in a circle;

sometimes we perform movements in unison; at other times we improvise exchanges of action, gesture and sound.

Around the time we were doing this research work, I often went out walking. On one cold day in late autumn, when the leaves had almost all gone and the trees stood with bare branches, I walked along the Boulevard Saint Michel in the Latin Quarter. I was carrying a bag of roasted chestnuts inside my coat in order to keep warm. When I had first walked down the same street about two and a half years before, it had been in the middle of the May revolution. Fierce fighting between students and police had taken place on this very spot. Now, the quietness of the street was in sharp contrast to my memory. Somehow it made me question myself. 'What will I become?' I thought. This peculiar uncertainty took hold of my emotions, creating all sorts of doubts and fears. The trees on the avenue looked particularly bleak at that moment.

Walking along, I recalled talks I had often had with the novelist Yukio Mishima. On many occasions, he and I had discussed the possibility of committing suicide. (According to Japanese tradition, suicide is an honourable death, and is not associated with failure or any lack of courage, rather the reverse.) Mishima talked about suicide as a way of drawing people's attention to certain points of principle. For myself, I had considered it because, at that time, I could see no real purpose in continuing to live.

Not long afterwards, I went to have breakfast with Peter. He was reading a newspaper, and he suddenly said, 'Do you know Yukio Mishima?'

'Yes,' I replied.

'He has committed hara-kiri.'

'I knew he would do it!'

I really resented my own stupidity at that moment. Why hadn't I tried to see him once more before I left Japan? I should have guessed from our final conversation that he was planning to commit suicide quite soon. For some peculiar reason, I had assumed it would happen in 1971. I foolishly thought that I would have one more chance to see him before he died.

I recalled my final contact with Mishima. Up until the day before my departure for Europe, I had been performing in a solo play written by Masaki Dohmoto, one of Mishima's followers. I played the role of a gigolo bartender, and Mishima himself had recommended me for this part. On the last night, Mishima's wife sent me a parcel. In it there was a fair amount of cash (it is a Japanese custom, called 'Senbetsu', to give money as a going away present), traditional summer clothing made of linen, and a letter, hand-painted with a brush.

'Even in the Capital of England, London, I would like you to wear this and not forget your Kamigata [Osaka area] spirit. To Oida kun, from Yukio Mishima.' (The title 'kun' is used instead of 'san' when referring to someone junior to yourself.)

Early the following morning, I visited Mishima's house. Mrs Mishima said that her husband was still in bed, so I asked her to convey my gratitude to him. Then I left the house for Haneda Airport, to board my flight to London. I was probably preoccupied by my own uncertain future, and was not able to perceive what was happening around me. I didn't realise that his letter was a Last Will and Testament to me, not simply a farewell note.

My first encounter with Mr Mishima was in 1965 when I joined the Bungaku-za theatre as a trainee. I attended the boxing club which was affiliated with the theatre, and which Mishima organised. But my enthusiasm for boxing lasted only a short while and I had no opportunity of speaking to him.

I met him again when he directed *Salome* by Oscar Wilde, the first and last time he directed the work of another author. I was given the part of the Young Syrian soldier. In no way could I have described myself as a good actor at that time. I did not know why I had been given such a major role. (The Young Syrian is deeply in love with Salome, and confesses his feelings towards her, but she rejects him. After learning that Salome is in fact in love with Jokaanan, he stabs himself in the chest and dies in despair.)

Before starting rehearsals, I was shown my costume which gave me a nasty shock. It consisted of shorts, boots, and sleeves. The chest and thighs would be completely exposed! At that time, I was very thin and had absolutely no confidence in my physical appearance. I immediately rushed up to Mishima to ask for help. He said, 'You can be my apprentice. Come with me.'

We went to a gymnasium called Sankei Body Building, under the railway arches in Yurakucho (in Tokyo). From then, until the opening of the play three months later, I worked solidly at building up my body.

During the rehearsals, when we were working on the scene of the soldier's suicide, Mishima complained to the set design people that there was not enough blood to make the moment visually striking. 'Produce more blood! There's too little blood.'

He said to me, 'The supreme death is sudden death during the sexual act. In that respect Salome was fortunate. She was given the head of Jokaanan whom she loved so passionately, and at the moment she reached the peak of her ecstasy, she was killed by the king.'

Ten years afterwards, when I heard of Mishima's sudden death, I finally realised why I had been given that major role, despite my lack of ability. People in the theatre company had often said that I physically resembled Mishima. Mishima himself knew this. He probably wanted to observe objectively how the act of suicide would appear to an onlooker, by using someone who resembled himself, as a sort of rehearsal. The next step he took was to perform a scene of hara-kiri himself in the film called *Yukoku*. He used the guts of a pig to create the effect of disembowelling. The third step was his actual suicide in the real world.

53

After *Salome* finished, I continued with bodybuilding, and Mishima often invited me to the Suehiro, a famous restaurant in the Ginza district, in order to treat me to beef steaks. He said:

'Bodybuilders are really strange people. All they are interested in is their muscles. I had a dinner party once, and after the beer had been served, they asked me to wait five minutes before serving the meal itself. Their reason was that since the gastric juices had been diluted by the drink, they could not digest the meal in full, therefore the precious food would be wasted. They won't have sex since they don't want to waste the protein. Wha ha ha ha ha!' He roared with his famous laugh.

'Look at novelist so and so, he is so thin, but still he thinks of himself as some sort of ladies' man. It is awfully foolish of women to fall in love with men for their intelligence. This kind of man believes that intelligence can make up for a lack of muscles. It really is a laughing matter. These men write in order to hide their problems with sex.

'Do you know that real males and females can never be good actors and actresses? The good actor has to be in a sense homosexual. Look at Sugimura [a famous actress]. She is a woman all right, but at the same time she is like a man. She knows what femininity is from a man's point of view. She is constantly aware of herself in front of men's eyes. Compared to her, the actor so-and-so is simply a male. Although he looks masculine in ordinary life, he lacks attractiveness on the stage, because he does not know what it is in him that women are attracted to. An actor should inwardly become a woman. They should play the kind of man a woman would fall for.

'You do not know how to act the super-star. If you pulled a funny face while Sugimura was acting superbly, the audience would look at you. In the film, the director decides whose face should be in close-up. On the stage, the audience is left to choose which one they want to look at. If you manage to attract the attention of the audience on the stage, even if you don't have a line to say, you could become a star.'

Around this time, we often talked about committing suicide in order to make a political point, but we couldn't agree about the method to use. In 1970, there was a demonstration organised against the celebration of the Emperor's birthday. Mishima went out to observe this event. I was very worried that he might choose to commit suicide as a protest against the demonstrators, since he was well known for his nationalistic views. However, the demonstration ended quietly, and I felt relieved. Later in 1970, there were more demonstrations organised by people protesting against the signing of the American–Japanese Peace Treaty. Unlike similar demonstrations in 1960 which had been very violent, these were moderate and calm. And so Mishima went on living.

One day, when it was so hot that you desperately longed for an air-conditioner, Mishima treated me to a meal in a Korean restaurant in Nogisaka called Hama. I told him about my plan to leave Japan, and about doing theatre research with Peter Brook for three years. He said: 'Don't say anything about your plans to anybody. Japan is a horrible place. You never know what people will do out of their jealousy. To avoid being pecked to death by them, you should leave quietly. Of course I don't mind at all. Not at all. Feel safe with me. For me, everything has already finished.'

That was the last conversation I had with Mishima.

When I was told of his death by Peter Brook, I did not feel sad. On the contrary, I envied him. My sadness was for the people left behind. As for Mishima himself, he did what he wanted to do. He committed suicide exactly as he had wished. In other words, he realised his dream. Yet I was not able to kill myself. I felt that I was a cowardly failure.

'Hey there, Oida! I have done it. Why are you still fooling around down there?' I imagined Mishima saying this with a cynical smile on his face.

I read many newspaper reports on the reasons for Mishima's suicide. It seemed everybody had got it wrong. I felt that the real circumstances that led to his suicide would not emerge for some time, if at all. Death comes to everybody eventually. Some people choose to carry on through the natural span of their lives, until death comes towards them. Others prefer to run towards it and meet it directly. I felt that Mishima must have had some kind of special experience that led him to choose the second path.

In 1981, eleven years after his death, I was staying in Besançon in eastern France, near Zurich. At that time, when I wasn't working on a play, I used to invite Japanese priests, both Buddhist and Shinto, to come to Europe for workshops to introduce European actors and dancers to some of the physical and mental disciplines of the two religions. For the workshop in Besançon, I invited Noboru Kobayashi, a Shinto priest from the Ishiyama Shrine. The training took place in this quiet town, enclosed in the mountains and valleys.

After the day's work, relaxing over a drink, we often chatted, talking about anything that came into our minds. One day the conversation touched upon Mishima. Mr Kobayashi said: 'When I was at the Ishikiri Shrine in Nara, Mr Mishima came to visit the shrine to do research for his book *Eirei no Koe* [The Voice of the Soldier's Ghost]. I was asked to take care of him. When I blew the ishibue [a stone flute] and explained that it is a sound for welcoming the spirits of heroes, he looked most touched. He stayed two or three days in the shrine. I would never have dreamed that he would end his life as he did.'

Then I said: 'Thinking about it, he died on the 24th of November, and that is tomorrow's date. Mr Kobayashi, would you mind holding a service for him before we start the workshop?'

Mr Kobayashi replied that Mishima had made a deep impression on him. He felt that meeting me, who had known Mishima well, was some kind of karma. He began writing a special prayer right away and suggested starting the ceremony at eight o'clock the following morning.

The next day, we constructed an altar, put offerings on it, and then started the service. The words of the service were in classical Japanese, in the distinctive style used by Shintoism. While listening to these words, I felt completely lost. The words evoked strong, typically Japanese emotions, which I found incongruous in this foreign situation.

Returning to Paris in 1970, the CIRT started work in its new studio. It was surrounded by stone walls, and initially created a rather cold atmosphere. But gradually it became familiar to us. We laid about twenty square feet of carpet, and put a circle of cushions round the edge. Inside that created space, we played and discussed. That was our style. Of course it was originally Peter Brook's idea. He said that true communication is impossible while people sit in chairs and talk across tables. But to many European members of the group, sitting on the floor was unfamiliar, and not particularly easy to do. I think the problem was caused by the fact that Westerners are extremely clever in organising their daily lives. When something proves difficult for them, they go and invent a completely new way of doing it! Japanese people are trained to sit on their knees from childhood by their parents. Naturally, it is difficult for anyone to sit for long periods on the floor, but in Japan they just keep on doing it until it eventually becomes easier. In contrast, Westerners prefer a lifestyle without excessive pain, and so they decided to invent the chair! The same thing occurs in music. It is not easy for fifty musicians to play a piece of music in unison, without sounding ragged. In Japan, musicians train themselves from childhood using special rhythmic exercises, so that everybody can sense the exact tempo, and the key moments in the piece. In the West, they invented a conductor to do this job. Orientals keep on persevering until the problem is solved. But when Europeans come across difficulties, they simply invent a new, easier method.

When I was leaving Japan, a famous writer said to me, 'Don't give up in the middle. The most important thing in seeking precious stones is to dig uncompromisingly until you reach the gems. If you keep on digging the same hole, you are bound to reach them eventually.'

This moved me deeply. This is truly 'Geido' (the way of art). 'Budo' (the way of martial art), 'Chado' (the way of tea), and 'Kado' (the way of the flower) are all based on this idea. The culture of repeated efforts.

Contrary to this, Brook's method is to seek another solution immediately if you are not making progress with an exercise. Although the work often appeared to be all right to me, given a bit more training or practice, he prefers to find another method to solve the problem. If I apply this to the writer's theory, he digs many holes instead of sticking to one. On reflection, I think the possibility of success is probably the same whether you are searching vertically (continuing to dig deeper into the same hole), or horizontally (digging another hole in a different place). It is a matter of whether you prefer to follow an absolute value in believing that the precious stone can only be found in that particular hole, or to make a relative value judgement; wherever you dig, the probability of finding gems is more or less the same.

There was an episode I heard of concerning the father of my Kyogen master. In the early days of recording, he was listening to his own performance which he had just recorded with the NHK (Japanese National Radio). The staff of the NHK asked him whether the recording was all right. His answer was: 'Yes, it's fine. Because it sounded just like my father.'

In a sense it is often easier if you believe in an absolute value; that there is only one correct way to follow, only one place to dig. However, there is something that must not be overlooked; whichever way you choose, there has to be a will to seek the precious stone at the bottom of the hole. The desire to 'dig' must be present, whichever way you wish to approach the work.

Brook often commented, 'Yoshi, you did that part very well today. What are you going to do tomorrow?'

In my opinion, if it was done well, then so be it. To seek another way for tomorrow seemed a bit of a waste of effort.

One day Brook said to me, 'You should stop using Japanese classical techniques from now on.'

As a Japanese actor, I was completely at a loss. What on earth would I do if I couldn't use my special Japanese techniques, especially while working among all these foreign actors? Of course, there are many ways to act, but there is no guarantee that I would be able to act well, if I was forced to use an unfamiliar technique. You can perform much better by looking into your own cupboard for the methods you have already used successfully in the past. You also feel secure with them. If I had to abandon my habitual techniques, kept deep in my cupboard, it meant that I had to put myself back at square one. Then what did this say about everything that I had acquired through years of training? Was my accomplishment there to be thrown away?

In Brook's opinion, the acting techniques being used in television and commercial theatre are often so skilful that they make brilliant imitations of life. But, like food in tins, they cannot be 'fresh' at the same time. What is needed onstage is the real vigour of life; the freshness. For this, you have to discard everything you have achieved, and stand on the stage without any preconceptions. Then you try to make something happen. But then, if nothing happens, you just make a fool of yourself. What is left to this actor called Yoshi Oida, when all the adjectives such as 'Japanese', 'having trained in traditional theatre', 'wearing the kimono', 'speaking Japanese', had been stripped away? I felt as if I was being thrown into the ocean, and left to float helplessly, clinging to a piece of timber.

However, as I discovered, the creative act can happen when one is denied and restricted in every direction. By limiting my technical vocabulary, Brook forced me to find a new theatrical language. In theory, the reverse ought to be true; you should feel most creative when all the restrictions are taken away, when you can do whatever you want. But, in practice, this often leads to confusion or inertia. In some ways, the more restrictions you have, the easier it is to work creatively. Because you know that certain 'well-dug' areas are off-limits in your 'digging for gems', you must find new territory to explore.

Learning to work with restrictions was difficult at first. Once all the techniques I had learned in Japan were prohibited, I had to switch my mind. The only things amongst my old methods that I could employ (without being spotted in superficial movements), were the basic approaches and concepts that lay hidden within the traditional styles of theatrical expression. In this way, I started to re-examine what I had learned from Noh.

Many years before, I had asked an eminent Noh critic, 'What is Noh?' He answered me in the following way:

Noh-gaku [the full name for Noh theatre] is a stage show where actors slowly move around the stage with small, shuffling steps. Nowhere else in the world does acting contain this. On the surface, what is expressed is minimal. The audience has to appreciate Noh by using their imagination, and their imaginations are invoked by small, minimal expressions which merely suggest the underlying emotions. Therefore Noh is an exceedingly tedious experience for people lacking imagination.

Despite the fact that Noh theatre employs a very slow-moving, minimal style of performance, it somehow manages to

60

engage the attention of the audience. To achieve this, it uses certain concepts which create a sense of inner movement and theatrical development. One of these is a rhythmic pattern called Jo-Ha-Kyu.

When I teach workshops, I often do an exercise which illustrates this idea. A group of people sit together with eyes closed, and start to clap their hands in unison. At first, the tempo of the clapping is slow and regular, then it gradually speeds up, and once it reaches a certain very fast speed, it peaks, and then resumes its original slow tempo. Eventually, it starts to gradually accelerate again. This pattern continues until the group is told to stop. If you ask the group why they did it, they answer that it was spontaneous.

This accelerating rhythmic pattern which passes through three different tempi (slow, middle, and quick) is constantly repeated in our ordinary life. A person's day usually starts slowly, towards midday work gathers momentum and continues through the afternoon. At dinnertime, we enjoy relaxing and chatting about the day's events and then we go to bed. Awakening of the spring, fertility of the summer, harvesting of the autumn, and repose of the winter. Even in lovemaking, the same rhythm can be seen. In China and Japan, this pattern is called 'Jo' (slow; or intro-ductory), 'Ha' (middle; unfolding), and 'Kyu' (fast; ending and conclusion).

This is the musical rhythm of Asian agricultural people. In India, China, and Japan it is the same. Gagaku (Japanese traditional music) has this pattern. It is in contrast to musical rhythms suggested by the regular beats of a heart, which keep a constant rhythm. (The heart-beat may be the pattern underlying the rhythmic music of the hunting peoples of Africa.) When a group of people clap together, everyone produces the Jo-Ha-Kyu pattern spontaneously. This suggests that the rhythm exists innately within us, and can be used to form a natural timing pattern for theatre. We often see, in a so-called 'artistic play', a

61

character monotonously using deliberately slow or restlessly quick movements. I must say that, for me, that actor is depicting an unrealistic person.

Zeami, the founder of Noh, wrote in the early fifteenth century:

> If we look attentively, all phenomena in the universe, all the acts of virtue and vice, things with feeling and without feeling, everything innately has this law of process 'Jo-Ha-Kyu'. From the chirping of the birds to the sounds of insects, everything sings according to their own law. And this law is Jo-Ha-Kyu. This is the reason why we find musical feeling in the sounds of birds and insects, feel something inspiring in them. If there were no law of unfolding and conclusion, surely we would not find these natural phenomena interesting or inspiring. When we perform one day's Noh [A traditional Noh programme consisted of five plays presented in a single day], the audience praises us at the end, since that day's Jo-Ha-Kyu has been completed. And in each individual play, there is the completion of the Jo-Ha-Kyu. Even a single dance or a single song appeals to us, because it has the rhythmic unfolding and conclusion of the Jo-Ha-Kyu pattern. And in a simple movement of a hand in the dance, and the sound of moving feet, we can find the law of Jo-Ha-Kyu. It appeals to the audience, since, in the act of appreciating a play, there is also the law of Jo-Ha-Kyu. Thus a play which moves the audience is made through the law of the Jo-Ha-Kyu which has been followed by the actors.

In terms of theatrical narrative, the 'Jo' section is introductory; it initiates the audience into the world of the play, and starts the action. 'Ha' changes the feel of the play, elaborates details, and generally develops the themes. 'Kyu' is the ending of the action.

62

If we look at *Hamlet* in terms of 'Jo-Ha-Kyu', it can be structured in the following way.

Hamlet meets the ghost of his father, understands what has happened, and then swears vengeance. Up until this point is 'Jo'. The next section is 'Ha', where he worries, hesitates, and philosophises. When he comes to a decision to fight, he moves into 'Kyu', which is the final section of duels. *Macbeth* also follows a similar structure. Macbeth meets the witches, and as a consequence kills the king. This is 'Jo'. Then the theme is developed with more killings, madness, and conflict. This is 'Ha'. The final section of the play, involving fast, strong scenes of battle, is 'Kyu'. But it is important to realise that the 'Kyu' section of a play does not always involve high-speed action, although this is fairly common. In fact, the visible activity might be quite slow. What makes it 'Kyu' is the fact that the interior energy of the scene remains very strong and active. 'Kyu' is energy, not merely speed.

Discovering all this was tremendously exciting. By denying me the use of my learned techniques, Brook had helped me unearth one of the key ideas of Noh theatre. It also proved to be a universally useful theatrical tool, and I began exploring ways of applying Jo-Ha-Kyu in all sorts of different exercises. Around this time, in the first year of the CIRT, Peter also started talking to the group about the use of Jo-Ha-Kyu. We have continued to employ it in various improvisations and productions ever since.

When Peter was structuring *The Mahabharata*, he consciously used the Jo-Ha-Kyu principle, and divided the piece into three sections. The beginning, entitled 'The Game of Dice', was 'Jo'; the second part, 'In the Forest', was 'Ha'; and the final section, 'The War', was 'Kyu'. Each section was then further sub-divided into a further Jo-Ha-Kyu. In the first part, the introductory section up until the birth of the two families was 'Jo'. The various relationships and detailed problems were 'Ha'. The actual scene of the dice-game was 'Kyu'; the 'Kyu' of 'Jo', to be precise. And so on.

These rhythms also affect the style of acting. It is not natural that Hamlet always stays in the same state, or at the same level of energy throughout the play. To remain true to life, acting needs to vary. So Peter might say: 'Don't always stay the same. You have to develop.'

In this way, at the beginning of *The Mahabharata*, you might try to play your character lightly. While in the final section, full of anger, vengeance, and destruction, you need to call on big, powerful emotions. The principle of 'Jo-Ha-Kyu' helps actors to structure their feelings, actions, and speeches in a natural way.

At the end of 1970, the CIRT group decided to produce a Christmas show for children. This was our first attempt at a public performance. During the rehearsals for the RSC *Midsummer Night's Dream*, Peter had taken the cast to a secondary school to find out how clearly the actors could communicate the story to children. This had proved to be an extremely valuable exercise. Actors sometimes go over the top, and tend to perform for their own artistic satisfaction, while leaving the audience behind. However, as Charlie Chaplin shows in his films, a performance may convey social, political, and philosophical messages, but still be interesting for children. Bearing this in mind, we tried to develop a play which had a similarly wide scope. Brook's main aim was to produce a play which could be enjoyed by everyone, from children to grown-ups, by workers as well as intellectuals. But whatever else we explored in the play, we had to maintain an easily comprehensible storyline, since we were playing specifically to an audience of children. We could not mystify them with philosophy, or ideological concepts. Having children as an audience was a good test for discovering whether our general aim of 'theatre-for-everyone' was being fulfilled.

The play we chose for the Christmas show was taken from a

nursery book. It was a story of a man who lives with bees. A French singer, Jacques Higelin, took the role of the narrator, and Robert Lloyd, an English actor, played the part of the Bee-Man. The story was told very simply by the other actors, using bamboo sticks, balloons and our fictional language, Bashta-hondo. However, in this play I was given my first line in French: 'Que voulez-vous, Monsieur?' Onstage, however, nobody could understand what I said, because of my terrible pronunciation!

During the play, the audience walked round the studio (which we had decorated with streamers and coloured paper), following the action as it moved from place to place. The show went well, and the children seemed to understand and enjoy it.

After all the performances had finished, we started to tidy up our studio, taking down the colourful strips of paper, red, blue, yellow, green, rolling them up like hanging scrolls. The cheerful theatre, covered with bright decorations, slowly changed back into the cold, stone-walled workshop.

'Now the shows have finished, it makes us feel sad somehow, doesn't it?' I said to Brook.

'Yes, it is sad. But since there is an end, we can now go on to the next step,' he replied.

'Damn! Why didn't I think of that myself!'

4 Holy Theatre – Orghast

In June 1971, the CIRT departed for Iran to prepare for our first big public performance. Up until then, we had conducted most of our work behind closed doors. Now, we wanted to test our research in an actual theatrical situation, and to let people see what we were doing. Peter had received an invitation from the Shiraz Festival, organised under the auspices of the Queen of Iran. (This was not part of the notorious celebrations that the Shah organised the following year.) The Queen was trying desperately to create a slightly liberal opening in the oppressive regime, and for a time the Shiraz Festival became a tiny window onto the outside world. Brook temporarily moved our base to Iran, enabling us to absorb Persian culture while working with Iranian musicians and actors. It also offered the group the opportunity of exploring Brook's idea of 'holy theatre'. He says in *The Empty Space*:

> I am calling it the Holy Theatre for short, but it could be called 'The Theatre of the Invisible-Made-Visible'; the notion that the stage is a place where the invisible can appear has a deep hold on our thoughts . . . More than ever, we crave for an experience that is beyond the humdrum. Some look for it in jazz, classical music, in marijuana and in LSD. In theatre, we shy away from the

66

holy because we don't know what this could be – we only know that what we call the holy has let us down . . . All the forms of sacred art have certainly been destroyed by bourgeois values, but this sort of observation does not help our problem. It is foolish to allow a revulsion from bourgeois forms to turn into a revulsion from needs that are common to all men; if the need for a true contact with a sacred invisibility still exists, all possible vehicles must be re-examined.

Persia is where West and East divide, and is the birthplace of many cultural elements which travelled to both Asia and Europe. It can even be described as an originating point for world culture. I thought it would be invaluable for our group to conduct research on theatre in this region which has great geographical and historical significance. It also would be very interesting to visit small villages in Iran where the majority of the people had never been to a theatre and therefore had no preconceptions about it. In performing there, we might be able to explore the basic meaning of theatre.

Since few people would fund this kind of activity simply out of interest, there was a string attached to the invitation. The requirement was to put on a performance for the rich and the intellectual classes of Iran as well as for visitors from Europe, as a part of the Shiraz Festival. Some of the members of the group objected. Their point was that the Shah of Iran had been keeping back revenue from the oil industry for his own use. He was going to spend some of this money on inviting 'artists' from Europe to the festival, for the entertainment of the bourgeoisie, instead of sharing this wealth with the poor. Some of our actors felt that it was wrong for us to conduct our activities using this 'dirty' money. Many other European and American artists and companies actually turned down their invitation to perform over the issue, and we were forced to confront this difficult question.

There was something about CIRT from the beginning that never ceased to astonish me. Theatre people had been gathered from all over the world and were paid to do research on the project, 'What is Theatre?' It was a great privilege, but to me, as a Japanese, it seemed strange that there were people who would sponsor this extravagant idea. In fact, the funds came from the French Government, the Rockefeller Foundation, Ford, the Anderson foundation, etc. It is more or less impossible to do any type of conscientious or exploratory work, if you are funded only by box office receipts. For our sort of theatre work, you need patrons of some kind. Indeed, it had taken several years of fund-raising activities to start this three-year research programme. Thanks to this funding, we could work full time on the project without worrying about money.

Since I first left Japan, I have met many people who are known as 'great artists'. I have found that these people possess diplomatic skills as well as artistic gifts. Previously, I had believed that an artist should be content with poverty, and that it was somehow un-artistic to think about money. I have now reached a different conclusion. An artist should not be content with poverty, yet he should be free to do creative activity without being obsessed by it.

My vote was for accepting the funding from the Shiraz Festival. In my mind, if our work went beyond materialistic concerns, and attained some higher level, then we could put ourselves outside the controversy, despite the fact that the money originated in the exploitation of people, and despotism.

We set off for Iran. Until that tour, my idea of foreign countries meant Korea, China, Europe and the UK. I had almost forgotten that there were other nations. When I arrived in Teheran, I went out into the streets. To my great astonishment, all the names of the streets were written in Arabic! In the taxis, even the numbers were written in Arabic! I also found

Sanskrit. I had forgotten that there were scripts other than Chinese, Japanese and the Roman alphabet.

In Iran, wealthy people dressed in European clothing, but the populace still dressed in the traditional style. The modernisation of Iran seemed slow, I thought. The same impression hit me when I went to visit African countries. I was surprised by what I mistakenly assumed to be their stubbornness in continuing to wear their traditional costumes. The ordinary Japanese lifestyle changed radically within a few years of having opened our country to the West. The old hairstyle of long hair bound into a topknot was soon regarded as barbarous, and the Government itself banned this style. The changes were brought in surprisingly swiftly.

However, my attitude to the notion of modernisation was to be re-examined. It happened in Paris, sitting in a taxi, while I was having a casual conversation with the driver. He said, 'Recently I went back to my country for the first time in ten years.'

'Where is your country?'

'Nigeria.'

'Well, I went to Nigeria several years ago. How was it over there? Was it more civilised than ten years before?'

'Civilised? What are you saying? Our country was "civilised" a long time ago, to the extent that there is no room to be more civilised!'

I was dreadfully ashamed that I had asked such a question.

This made me challenge my previous notion that 'civilisation' and 'modernisation' meant blindly accepting European attitudes. On the other hand, I have sometimes been criticised for maintaining my own cultural habits. One of my Japanese friends visited our centre, and saw me wearing the kimono. He said, 'I was ashamed to see you wearing traditional costume. It was as if you were using Japanese exoticism as your selling point.'

I thought I understood his objection and changed into a

69

T-shirt and tracksuit trousers. Brook immediately said that this was a bad European influence. True, I thought, my initial choice was correct. Why do people all over the world imitate European clothes, as if they were an easy solution? If the kimono is truly inconvenient, why not design something completely new? It is wrong to think that if you have copied European customs and philosophies, you will be all right anywhere in the world. Besides, the kimono is an ideal garment for movement.

As well as working on 'holy theatre', Brook wanted to explore 'rough theatre' while we were in Iran. In *The Empty Space*, Peter describes 'rough' or 'popular' theatre in the following way:

> Through the ages it has taken many forms, and there is only one factor that they all have in common – a roughness. Salt, sweat, noise, smell: the theatre that is not a theatre, the theatre on carts, on wagons, on trestles, audience standing, drinking, sitting round tables, audiences joining in, answering back: theatre in back rooms, upstairs rooms, barns: the one-night stands, the torn sheet pinned up across the hall, the battered screen to cover the quick changes . . . the rough theatre is close to the people . . . it is usually distinguished by the absence of what is called style.

We decided to put on a performance in a rural village. In Iran at the time, these were very closed communities. There were no televisions, and we were warned that the villagers might attack us with their hoes when they saw that their village was being 'invaded' by a pack of strangers. So we practised retreating to our bus, using a stop-watch to time our exits. By the end of our training, we were able to make extremely speedy departures!

The play we took with us was a comic sketch about family problems. The basic story was narrated by an Iranian television star, but we spoke in our own created language, Bashtahondo. And because in Iran women were prohibited from appearing in public without a veil, we decided to respect local custom and have the women's roles played by male actors. The women members of the CIRT came along, and sat at the edge of the carpet making music.

We arrived near the village when it was already dusk, and the villagers were coming home from the fields. When we rather cautiously entered the village, people glared at us, and all the women and children ran away and hid in their houses. There was cattle dung everywhere, and the place stank. All the peasants lived together with their cattle, and it looked as if the cows were part of the family. The tense waiting went on for a little while, but eventually a man, who seemed to be the Head of the village, approached us and asked why we had come.

'We are tourists who have come to see your village, but we are also actors. If you agree, we would like to perform something for you. Will you let us do that?'

To our surprise, the village chief accepted our offer straight away.

We spread a carpet we had brought with us on top of the mountain of dung, and started to perform our (literally) 'Stinker of a Play'. In the beginning, the audience only consisted of men, but gradually women and children started to gather round.

It was an ordinary comedy using themes from daily life. But since the audience was very closed and unresponsive, we had no idea whether or not it was working. Afterwards, because people had been attracted to the show and remained to watch, we assumed it had been successful. But while we were acting, we hadn't a clue, especially since it was our first attempt at performing this style of popular theatre, where the story was half-scripted, half-improvised. Nonetheless, it was a valuable experience since it introduced us to the kind of work we would develop in our African journey the following year. In Africa, we travelled from village to village, performing on our carpet (which became a kind of mobile 'stage'). In fact, our show in Iran was the very first 'Carpet Show'.

After the show, Peter said to me, 'Your acting is too concentrated and strong for this style of work.'

I realised that I was still performing in accordance with the principles of Noh theatre where the actor's concentration must be extremely intense. But popular theatre requires another approach. And I realised that just as there are many levels of performance, there is no one 'right' way to act.

I also felt that theatre could tell us a great deal about communication between people of different nationalities. Through acting, we could learn from the audience and make certain discoveries, as well as offering entertainment to them. I felt that 'living theatre' actually existed in a place like that.

The date for the main public performance gradually approached. People were coming from all over the world to find out what Brook was doing, as well as to see the work of other innovative companies and artists. It would be a tremendous event, and Peter chose a spectacular setting for our show, which was called *Orghast*.

We performed in Persepolis, among the ruined tombs of Darius and Xerxes. Persepolis was where the glorious Persian civilisation had flourished, prior to its destruction by Alexander the Great in the fourth century BC. Now only the ruins of the tombs, temples and palaces remain. The first part of the play was performed at sunset, in front of the tomb of King Artaxerxes II, carved into the rockface behind the palace. The second part was performed at Naqsh-el-Rustam, where Darius I and II and Xerxes I and Artaxerxes I are buried. This was performed at sunrise. *Orghast* was written by the English poet, Ted Hughes. It was based on Greek mythology, and the stories of Prometheus, Hercules and Oedipus were combined.

The script was written in a new, complete language called 'Orghast', created by Ted Hughes. This was a real language, with each word having a specific meaning, unlike Bashtahondo which was a collection of nonsense sounds whose meaning would shift according to the intentions of the actor. Since none of us understood this language, Hughes translated it into English, and then each of us in turn translated it into our native language, word by word, so that we could follow the storyline. After this, we used Hughes's language for rehearsals. In addition, we used classical Greek text from the tragedies of Prometheus and Oedipus, Latin from Seneca, and also Avesta, the sacred language used over two thousand years ago in ancient Persia. All of these were dead languages, and, like our created language, would not be understood by the audience. A few people might understand Greek or Latin, but no one could understand all of the languages employed in the production.

In general, oral language contains many elements. The first is the transmission of information to another person. 'One and one equals two', 'My name is Oida', 'I like you' etc. The second is a musical effect, like in jazz, 'Bi-bop bi ba'. The third element is incantation or mantra, like 'amen', 'ohm'. Mantras are words or phrases which are believed to connect human beings to the energy of the universe, and have a supernatural effect. It seems that in ancient times, rain fell when the incantation of 'Rain' was uttered, and a man would die when a spell was cast. Nowadays, nothing happens if someone says 'Rain' or 'Die'. Words and their power have become separated. However, in 'Orghast', our task was to reconnect words to the inner feeling. If I uttered the word created by Ted Hughes which meant 'rain', then it should start raining. This required a completely different style of delivery to the one normally used in modern plays. The actors had to find ways of dredging up real power and intensity in their voices, since we wanted the audience to be shaken and moved by the primal strength of our created language. This was challenging, but also extremely exhausting!

None of the rehearsals for *Orghast* were particularly easy. To get to Persepolis from the hotel, we had to travel for one and a half hours in an old bus. The place was in the middle of the desert, and it was too hot to work in the daytime. Even though rehearsals started at dusk, you could still feel the heat coming off the rocks. The desert wind, blowing in the middle of this heat and aridity, drained all the energy from our bodies. Persepolis was situated at 1700 metres above sea level. When we spoke, we ran out of breath quite quickly, since the air was so thin. The sand carried on the wind was like smoke. If we inhaled it, it damaged our throats. If we drank water to quench our thirst, it caused diarrhoea.

'Militarism' was a word quite often used in Japan at that time. It means, I suppose, that a country is governed by a despot who uses armed force to back his rule. Iran was quite literally in this state. During rehearsals, soldiers with guns would walk across the stage whenever they felt like it. They were everywhere in the ruins, keeping an eye on us. The actresses were not even able to go behind the rocks for a pee.

Orghast opened on 28 August. Many members of the audience had come on a long journey from Europe or the USA. They flew to Teheran, took another plane to Shiraz, and then endured another bumpy hour and a half on a bus to the ruins of Persepolis. After this they faced a climb up to the tombs, which took about twenty minutes. We may have called this place a 'theatre', but in reality it was a ruined burial place. There was no stage and no curtain. Both the audience and the actors sat cross-legged on cushions, waiting for the sun to go down. When the sun was on the point of setting, the cue for the commencement of the piece was given. A huge ball of fire descended from the sky; Prometheus had stolen it in order to give fire to humankind. A man was about to accept the gift of fire, when a tyrant (which was the role I played) took it from him. The tyrant was the embodiment of evil, and the fire drove him mad. He started killing people one by one, ending in the murder of his own family.

74

The story we performed was created in an unusual way. We began the work in Paris, just doing general improvisations. Ted Hughes observed us and made some basic character decisions, such as, 'He would be good as a mad king', 'She suits the role of a queen'. Then he wrote a lot of stories in his invented language, using these characters. I had twenty stories, while Irene Worth had forty. The twelve actors probably had a total of about two hundred stories between them. We started to improvise, using these stories, and gradually we eliminated the ones that didn't work. Once we had a pool of stories that were theatrically interesting, Peter and Ted Hughes began to link them into a single, coherent epic. We also did some explorations using ancient Greek text, and if a particular section worked well, Peter retained it.

Later we visited the spot where we were to perform and decided where certain scenes needed to be placed. We agreed that this one needed to be staged on top of the tomb, while another needed to be performed on the ground. For the first section of *Orghast*, we decided that the audience would be seated, watching the action unfold in front of them, while the second part would be staged in several different areas. For this performance, the audience would be led about the ruins, observing each scene in its chosen setting. Our decisions about the space affected the relations between the characters, as well as defining the impact of each scene on the audience. The space also played an important role in the construction of the narrative: how did the story lead the audience from one location to the next? Because of the way the performance came together, nobody knew whether or not they had a 'leading' part. Everyone had their own stories, but only at the very end did the relative importance of those stories emerge.

Since the script was written in either newly-created or dead languages, the audience could not understand the literal meaning of the words we used. But they seemed to have little difficulty in following the action, communicated through movement and voices. In the end, when the tyrant realised he had murdered his own family, he blinded himself. He was then killed by his eldest son and left in the tomb. At that point, all the torches and candles were extinguished, leaving the clear light of the half-moon shining on the stage.

An enormous wave of applause broke out. People sat talking about the excitement of the play, in a field of ruins where there was no café. I stayed hiding in the cave of the tomb, looking up at the moon. Throughout my acting career, once every five or ten years, I felt the searing joy of being in the theatre. That was one of those moments. Except at these times, I always want to give up acting as a career.

One week later, the second part of *Orghast* opened at 4.30 a.m. at Naqsh-el-Rustam. The mad king (my role) descended into Hell after his death. He witnessed the historical events that had actually occurred at the place we were performing, over two thousand years before. The actors used lines written by the ancient Greek playwright Aeschylus, taken from his play *The Persians*. My character was witnessing history. As he moved from place to place among the ruins, the audience followed him. I found it strangely moving that a Japanese actor was praying to the gods in Greek, at the very spot where the Persians had begged the spirit of Darius to save them from Alexander.

The audience watched this event which was situated beyond the boundaries of time and space, where the distinction between past and present, East and West, evaporated. Finally, the mad king disappeared into the temple of the God of Fire. The sun started to rise. The birds woke and departed. Then a man went into the fields with an ox, which was our symbol of the spirit. The audience, who by then had started to feel sleepy, went back to their hotels on the rattling, bumpy buses. As I watched them leave, I thought about the play that had just finished.

Orghast was the first time since I had left Japan that I had performed a specific role in a play. The 1968 *Tempest* was an experiment which took fragments of Shakespeare and explored them, but *Orghast* was a story with a text, even though the audience couldn't understand the words.

In Japan, when I had performed Western-style theatre, the story was always about ordinary human events and feelings. In contrast, *Orghast* used strong, archetypal situations and powerful, unusual languages. The languages of Greek, Latin, Avesta, and Orghast had the same kind of vibrant energy that you find in Shakespeare. However, Shakespeare's language is related to the forms of Elizabethan theatre, and you must consider these forms when you act in his plays. Since *Orghast* was an invention, there were no forms to be observed. You could bring yourself to the play in any way that you chose.

While the characters related to each other in humanly truthful ways, I felt that there was a universal resonance to the action. This feeling was reinforced by the location. Playing the part of the King in front of the tomb of a real monarch who had died thousands of years before, made me aware that my words stretched through time to the past, and also to the future. Similarly, they were not bound by space. They could travel anywhere. I really understood what Peter meant by 'holy' theatre. I felt that *Orghast* touched something that was similar to ancient Greek theatre. The human actions on the stage were a microcosm of the universe.

Playing the story is not enough; we also need to look in other directions. If we look upwards, we see the broad expanse of the universe. If we look downwards, we see our ordinary daily reality, with its social, political, and economic problems. Between these two worlds, theatre must build a bridge. As actors, we need to be aware of the reality of the universe as well as the reality of everyday life. Some theatre companies perform what could be called 'political' theatre, in its narrow sense. But they are only looking at the details of social existence. Similarly, other styles of theatre only concern themselves with the universe, and, as a consequence, are cut off from what their audience actually experiences on a day-to-day basis. Even in Japan, there is a beautiful box called 'Noh theatre'. It has been polished by years of tradition, but it is a museum piece, linked to a world that is dead and gone. It can communicate on a universal level, but it no longer connects to what people experience in their ordinary lives today. In Iran, I felt that we had created a theatre that was trying to connect these two realities.

The two parts of *Orghast* were each performed for a week, with a gap in between. However, there was a special day set aside for the Queen of Iran. On that day, the first part was shown at dusk, and the second part two hours later, so that she would not have to make two separate journeys. The Queen arrived with many attendants, friends, and guards. The first half of *Orghast* went without a hitch. While the Queen was resting in a tea-house on the road to Persepolis, we drove to the other location in order to set up for the second half. We planned to have it ready before she appeared, but when we got there, we found it had been barricaded by the police. This was for the protection of the Queen, and when we tried to enter, the guards stopped us, saying, 'Nobody is allowed to enter.' Brook told the guards that we were the people that the Queen was coming to see, and therefore we needed to finish our preparations before she arrived. But the guard would not listen, and just kept insisting that no one was permitted to enter. We explained that we could not play if we didn't have the time to prepare for the performance. After a long argument we gave up and left the place.

The stupidity of the guard deeply upset us. We concluded that it was impossible to work in a country where military power has such control. We felt we should just pack up and return to Paris. We started to walk away from Persepolis along a narrow, single-track road in the desert. At that moment, the Queen's car appeared ahead of us. It was taking the Queen to see the second part of the show. Brook told us, 'Don't explode with rage. Keep calm and keep walking. Don't resist, whatever happens.'

The car stopped in front of us, and the Minister for Culture, who was also the Queen's elder brother, stepped out and asked us what was happening. Despite his warning to us, Brook was furious, and shouted that we were going back to Paris immediately. In the end, the Minister intervened, and Brook agreed to perform the second half. The show finally took place, several hours later than scheduled, when we were ready (and not before!).

Officially, the CIRT's research activities for the first year concluded with the *Orghast* project. The group split up, with many promises of reunion. The other actors were flying back to the West, while I alone flew eastwards. But even at Teheran airport the problems didn't end. At passport control I was stopped by police, and was about to be sent to jail. My visa had expired one day before, so officially I had stayed illegally in the country. Fortunately the Festival Director had accompanied me to the airport, and he phoned the Minister for Culture who arranged to have me released. I managed to leave for Japan that same day. Throughout the three-month stay in Iran, I had suffered from diarrhoea, and I had been tormented by the heat and aridity. I felt half-dead in the aeroplane, and my feet seemed to be galloping by themselves, rushing to get back to Japan as quickly as possible.

5 Rough Theatre – Conference of the Birds I

Back in Japan, I quickly recovered from the rigours of Iran, but I soon realised that I still had 'itchy feet'. I looked at my timetable, and decided to fit in a flying visit to America before returning to Paris for the re-opening of the CIRT in October. I had already been there once, after my initial visit to Paris, so this was my second time in America. The first time, I was just an ordinary tourist. The second time, I was treated like a Hollywood star. On arrival in California, I realised that the journalists and people in theatre circles already knew about me. The event in Iran had been given a lot of publicity in the *New York Times*, and I appeared quite prominently in the article. The welcome in New York was even greater, since that was the home-territory of the paper. It was amazing to realise that a single page in a newspaper article had changed people's ideas so drastically. Of course, it wasn't an unpleasant feeling, being treated as a star. But, objectively speaking, I don't think that my performance was that good. It was nonsense the way all these theatre people believed that I was a great actor, simply because a single critic had been impressed by my work.

Although it is natural in an age of mass communications, America's faith in critics has gone too far. On Broadway, a play may have cost tens of millions of dollars to mount, but if a critic from a big newspaper was short of sleep on opening night, and writes 'boring and tiring', then the play will fold immediately. The tens of millions of dollars evaporate into the air. Putting on a show becomes a mere gamble, and nothing is more foolish than that.

I went from New York to Paris for the second year of the CIRT research programme. The work of the first year focused on 'holy theatre', culminating in the performance in Iran. In the second year, the theme was completely different; the recovery of 'rough theatre'. We had begun to examine this area with our 'carpet show' in the village in Iran, but now we wanted to explore it in greater depth.

Our first project was *Kaspar Hauser*, based on the work of Peter Handke. The story was based on the experiences of a young boy who had been completely shut away from the world until the age of sixteen. He had no idea of human language or social behaviour. After he was discovered, he began to learn human language, how to walk, how to sit, how to wear clothes. Little by little he learned about society and its manners. After learning all this, he went mad. I thought this was a great play. It had the same impact on me as when I read *Waiting for Godot*, just after the Second World War. The question that *Godot* addressed was: 'How do we live in this world?' Fifteen years later when I encountered *Kaspar*, I felt it posed equally relevant questions.

We started to rehearse in autumn 1971. It was an extremely complex play, and initially we followed the text exactly. If it said 'Right foot forward', we moved the right foot. Then Peter began to extract and develop certain elements within the play. The piece we eventually created was based on Peter Handke's original play, but we did not follow the text. We performed for audiences consisting of polytechnic students, as well as visiting psychiatric hospitals, where we performed for both the patients and the professors. As well as these more 'sophisticated' audiences, we played at local youth clubs. Wherever we did the

show, the audiences were fascinated by this question of language, and its role in the acquisition of 'humanity'. Finally, we
performed in front of a theatrical audience, who also responded
extremely well.

The piece made people aware of the two sides of the human
being, the artificial side which is created in the social world, and
the original instinctive nature. Brook was asking the question,
'What is the instinctive human being?' and 'What happens as
that person acquires language, manners, physical comportment
and social awareness?' I feel that Peter is always looking for the
instinctive kind of response when he is directing. He doesn't just
play around with movement or language, but is looking for a
deeper level of human engagement. Peter never talks about the
spirit or the soul. Indeed, if you try to talk about it, the
discussion becomes rather artificial. But if you perform freely as
a basic human being, the spiritual element will naturally emerge.
Unfortunately, as actors, we tend to use the theatrical side of our
nature. Through this, you can produce interesting, exciting
performances, but you can't touch the spiritual side of the
human being. Peter is always looking for an alive, free, human
response. His approach in all the plays, including Shakespeare,
is not to communicate a specific message. Instead he encourages
the actors to explore the text or the original material in a
responsive, open, human way. Then various interpretations or
aspects naturally emerge. Out of these, the audience is free to
choose its own 'message'.

At the end, we invited Peter Handke to see our work. We did
two versions; the first was the free-form piece that we had
created. Half an hour later, we performed Handke's text,
exactly as it had been written. I don't know what Peter Handke
really thought about our freely adapted version, but he said that
he preferred it to the original!

To develop our research into 'rough theatre', Peter decided to
try placing our performances in an uncontaminated 'primordial'

environment – to play in front of audiences who had not been influenced by modern commercial theatre or television, and had no preconceptions about the nature of theatre. At the same time, there was another important theme. Peter seemed interested in observing the reactions of our group, whose membership was drawn from so many different cultural backgrounds, under special conditions. In addition, he wanted to do research on the story of *The Conference of the Birds*. This was a Sufi fable, which Peter wanted to explore as a piece of theatre. To pursue these aims, Brook decided to go to Africa.

As for myself, I didn't really want to go there. I had got used to the advantages of modern Western technology, such as central heating, flush toilets, and air conditioning. These didn't exist in Japan when I was young. I couldn't understand why all these Westerners wanted to experience such primitive conditions. I liked the comforts of Europe! But, since everybody was so keen to go to Africa, I decided to tag along.

On the 1st of December, we left Paris and embarked on a hundred-day tour of Africa. There were more than twenty of us in all, eleven actors, plus writers, musicians, director, and others. We flew to Algeria where we joined an English guide, cook, and mechanic. Then we headed south in four jeeps and a truck. Our route took us south from Algeria across the Sahara desert, to the Niger, Nigeria, then west to Benin and Mali, then north again, recrossing the Sahara to Algeria. The total distance was 16,000 kilometres.

North Africa, above the Sahara, is mainly inhabited by Muslim Arabs. However, one day as we were nearing the desert, we came across a town where there was a substantial black population. We discovered the reason for this. In the past, black Africans were traded as slaves by the Arabs, and were brought across the desert from the south. After the harsh journey across the Sahara, many were unable to travel any further, and were abandoned here by the slave traders. Their descendants now live in this area. I saw the heavy bracelets, which were originally fastened onto slaves to prevent them escaping, being sold in the market. And there were also sticks, like colourful Italian china, previously used as currency in the slave trade. They probably only cost a few pence to make, but human beings were traded with them.

To reach black Africa, we had to cross the Sahara desert. Natasha Parry, Brook's wife, told me that the desert changes people. From her words, I imagined it involved an interminable trek, but in fact, we managed to dash across the worst part of the desert in three days, travelling from oasis to oasis like stepping stones. We began our journey by crossing the Atlas mountains to Algeria. Then we entered the region of the Tuareg tribes. They carry swords, and mask their faces, which makes them look quite flamboyant. The approach to the Sahara consists of rolling sand dunes, but after you leave this region and enter the true desert, the sand vanishes and the ground becomes absolutely flat, like a tray. Between the point where I was standing on the rocky plain, and the horizon, there was nothing. Absolutely nothing. Only mirages, which looked like pools of water. For 360 degrees around, everywhere looked the same. The desert in December was as fresh as an autumn day. There was a gentle breeze on my cheeks, and the world of silence made me feel free.

I was born in Kansai (the Osaka area), but moved to Tokyo to escape the obligations of duty that are an inevitable part of family life in Japan. I then left Tokyo for Paris, partly to escape the wider obligations associated with being a member of Japanese society. However, even in Paris, where initially I had no social niche, I ended up being a part of a community. I am no longer a stranger there. But in the desert there was no society around me, only our small group. Inside my skin was 'me', outside there was only sky and earth. I remembered an old Chinese expression 'Ten, Chi, Jin' (Sky (Heaven), Earth, Human). Here in the desert, there was only sky and earth outside myself. I had always accepted the phrase as a concept, but now that I found myself in the actual situation, I didn't know how to physically place myself. I felt insignificant, a mere speck of dust. Standing was no good. It didn't feel right. So I tried lying down on the surface of the plain which was covered with small pebbles, rounded by the desert wind over time. I looked up at the sky. That position made me feel like a dead man. I was merely part of the desert soil. I did not have any individual existence. Next, I tried sitting up with a straight back. That wasn't bad. I remembered the words of the old Zen master, 'Concentrate your energy in your lower abdomen.' Sitting like that suddenly made me feel as if I truly existed between heaven and earth. At that moment, I found a new and very particular sense of my own existence. But this sense was nothing to do with my ordinary sense of being. It seemed to belong to me, and at the same time, it existed outside me. As a result of sitting there, my sense of being and existence had been somewhat altered. The desert had changed me after all.

Placing the spine horizontally on the earth means being asleep, being dead, not existing as a conscious being. Placing the spine vertically in relation to the earth means being alive, existing. Most animals, with the exception of humans, live with their spines horizontal to the earth. It is only the human race which has chosen to erect our spines vertical to the earth. Jesus Christ, Buddha, and Mohammed all had spiritual revelations while owning a vertical spine. I have never heard of anyone attaining full and conscious spiritual enlightenment while lying down. It seems that in order to contact a vast invisible energy, one has to place one's spine vertical to the earth. Human beings do not only exist between heaven and earth, they exist to connect heaven and earth.

The smell, the feeling, the taste, and the silence of the Sahara became deeply engraved on me. Those English gentlemen, our support team, were all graduates of famous universities. But in order to stay in the desert, they had chosen menial occupations. Or so I heard. Even I, who am not usually a keen traveller, would go back to the desert, if offered the chance. It is difficult to describe the attraction. Perhaps it is like being addicted to drugs. When you are away from the desert, withdrawal symptoms begin to appear, and you start to want to experience that special state again.

Early every morning in the desert, we would sit together in total silence. Most people found this exercise incredibly difficult for some reason. The company still continues to do this exercise. Before every performance, we sit together in silence as a group. It seems quite easy now. Maybe it is simply a question of practice, or maybe we are just not as young as we were in Africa!

As we journeyed south, we saw the other face of the desert. It was impossible not to be horrorstruck, witnessing the slow invasion of the desert at the northern edge of Nigeria, caused by the droughts of the previous few years. Trees were dying, and the roads were disappearing into the sand. As we travelled further south, the desert ended and we came across a village. The only inhabitants were eight women and children. Since there had been no rain and no harvest, all the men had gone south five years before to work as migrant labour. As I write now, sixteen years have passed. The village may have already vanished.

During the hundred days of the trip, I did not spend even one day under a roof or tent. I lay under the sky every night with just the folding bed and sleeping bag which had been issued to us all. We each used two litres of water a day for washing our bodies. This was the case throughout the tour, not only in the desert. Even near the Equator where there was plenty of water, it was difficult to be sure of its purity. Our food consisted of an English breakfast served by the cook, tinned food such as sardines or corned beef for lunch, and a hot meal in the evening. After my bad experience with diarrhoea in Iran, I didn't touch meat. I had

1 Yoshi in Kyogen, Tokyo, 1964

2 Yoshi as Krogon in *Orghast,* 1971

3 Yoshi as Atum in *The Ik*, 1975

4 Exercises at the CIRT, 1970/71.
L/R: Michele Collison, Yoshi,
Andreas Katsulas, Bruce Myers.
(Photo: Christopher Davies)

5 *Conference of the Birds*, 1979.
L/R: Maurice Benichou, Mireille Maalouf,
Miriam Goldschmidt, Yoshi,
Malik Bagayogo.
(Photo: Enquerand, Paris)

6 *Tibetan Book of the Dead,* Almeida Theatre, London 1990.
Yoshi and Elsa Wolliaston. (Photo: Ivan Kyncl)

7 *The Tale of the Chameleon,* Almeida Theatre, London 1990.
Koffi Koko and Yoshi. (Photo: Ivan Kyncl)

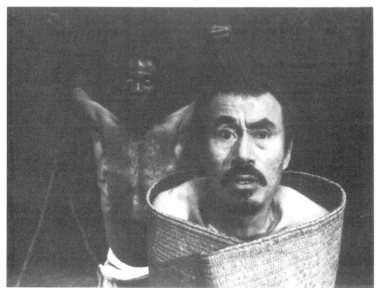

8 *Interrogations* – The Words of the Zen Masters, 1979.
(Photo: Aldo Agnelli, Milan)

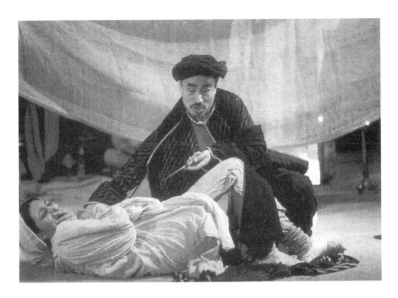

9 *The Mahabharata.*
Yoshi and Mallika Sarabhai.
(Photo: Gilles Abegg, Paris)

10 *The Mahabharata.*
Georges Carraface, Yoshi,
Andrzej Seweryn, Mamadou Dioume.
(Photo: Gilles Abegg)

11 *The Mahabharata,* 1985. Yoshi as Drona.

12 *La Tempête,* 1990. Tapa Sudana (back) and Yoshi.

also heard that if you don't eat meat, your body temperature becomes lower, and that this decreases the likelihood of getting malaria. Indeed, with the exception of myself, all the members of the group got malaria to some degree or another. I also managed to avoid diarrhoea.

Our first show was at In Sallah. After that, we performed whenever we found a suitable place. It could be the middle of a market, the centre of a village, wherever we saw a practicable spot. We just laid out our carpet and began to play on an impromptu basis. Within the hundred days of our tour, we managed to do more than thirty shows. Normally when we arrived in a village, the first thing we did was to ask the children to take us to the Head of the village. It is possible to communicate with children everywhere in Africa, since they learn either English or French (depending on which country originally colonised the area) at school. Once we had managed to find the Head of the village, we would ask permission to set up camp at the outskirts of the community. Then we would lead up to our offer: 'We are singers and dancers from all over the world. If you are interested, we would like to show you our song and dance. And we would also like to see something from you.'

There is no word meaning 'theatre' in Africa, so we described our activities in that way. Then we would agree a time for our show and their concert, and we would start to prepare. We never knew how large the audience would be. We have had as few as five, and also over a thousand, which greatly surprised us. As for the show itself, we had prepared quite a few in Paris. We tried them, one after another, but they did not appeal to the audiences. Plays made by the European intellect were very far away from the feelings of the local people. In one particular place, we tried everything we knew, but whatever we attempted, the audience showed no sign of interest, and the hum of their continuing conversation never subsided. Eventually we ran out of plays, and Brook asked me to sing a Japanese folk song. He also asked Michele Collison, an American actor, to sing something from the USA, the idea being that music has no national boundaries.

'Kiso no ma na-a, nakanori san', 'Summertime, and the living is easy'. Even with these, the audience still continued to chat, and showed no sign of interest. Finally, at our wit's end, Brook asked them to sing for us. They started to clap and sang a strange tune 'Ah – Ah – Ah – '. We asked for another. Again they started to clap, and sang a very similar tune. This reminded me that Japanese 'enka' (popular sentimental songs) all sound more or less the same. Brook said, 'Yes, clapping is common all over the world. 'Ah – Ah – Ah' is also an international language. Let's try it that way.'

But we didn't know how to do it. To begin with we clapped our hands, and some of us uttered the sound 'Ah – Ah', as if full of joy. Others made the sound as if they were full of rage, or weariness, or sadness. 'Ah – Ah – Ah'. Gradually, the audience became silent and started to listen attentively to our 'Ah – Ah – Ah' song. Great! We had started to get the knack of it! Then one of our French actors started to sing 'Ah – Ah – Ah' in the complex scale of modern music. Immediately the audience lost interest, and the buzzing of private conversation started up again. At that moment we realised that the essence of song is to express emerging feelings simply and melodically.

Those Japanese and American folk songs we initially tried seemed simple at first glance, but, in fact, they have already become too complex. They have lost the power to move all of us on a universal level. Too much attention goes into phrasing and details, and the true nature of the song has become lost. For a song of joy to be universal, it ought to be joy itself. The expression ought to be kept as simple as possible.

We had already thrown away the show we had worked on in Paris, and we were just improvising in front of the audience. One day, an American actor, Andreas Katsulas, put his boots in the middle of the carpet. Suddenly the people watching became interested in what was happening. In their culture, shoes symbolised power, success, wealth and the trappings of modern life. An actress stepped into the boots, and was transformed into an irresistible beauty. Another actor became a vain bully under their influence. The boots themselves changed people and precipitated conflicts, trickery and desire. These objects had enabled the actors to find something in common with the African audience. Every time we performed this 'Shoe Show' we began in the same way. The boots would be placed in the centre of the carpet. Then one of the actors would start to improvise with them, and other people would join in. Each time we did it, we would explore new ways of using and relating to the boots. It was never the same twice, but the audiences always responded to it. Because we were using an improvisational approach, the show often fell apart, but at least we had found a point of true contact.

Once we realised that we were on the right track, we started looking for another theme that would work in the same way. When you do pure improvisation, there is always a risk of falling flat on your face. Sometimes it works, sometimes it doesn't. To reduce this risk, Peter decided to construct a basic story, which was called the 'Bread Show'. One man sells bread. Another buys it. Other people try to steal it from him. This structure made it easier to improvise, but our work tended to become naturalistic as a result. Once we knew what would happen next, we focused on pushing the story along, rather than exploring the possibilities of each situation. It had become like an ordinary Western play. There wasn't enough energy in the performance, and the actors had got caught up in unnecessary surface details which had no meaning for the audience. To remedy this, we decided to do the show with music, using a rhythmic beat. We played the entire show in time to this pulse. It raised the energy of the performance and made it stronger, but we weren't very good at rhythmic work. We had a little rehearsal the next day, just practising with our hands and faces, and then played it that evening. This time it worked! ,

Afterwards, we usually discussed what things had worked and what hadn't. Each show we performed had to last forty-five minutes, and we discovered that forty-five minutes of pure improvisation is very hard to sustain. A basic structure made it easier, but this in turn created other problems, so we had to keep exploring. In the mornings, as part of our preparation for *The Conference of the Birds*, we would go to the trees and just listen to bird sounds. We started to imitate their movement patterns. We did some improvised conversations using bird noises in the place of speech. We even created a complete 'bird version' of *Romeo and Juliet*, where all of the characters were birds, and their calls were used in place of text. At other times, we returned to the idea of performing specific characters, such as 'The King', 'The Hag', 'Death', in order to see what sort of situations would develop through their interaction.

Since we didn't always want to use the 'Shoe Show' and the 'Bread Show', we developed a third performance called the 'Walking Show'. It began one day when none of us knew how to start the performance. A very tall American actor, Lou Zeldis, entered the carpet and started walking. He just walked. On and on and on. Eventually he turned into a bird, and then someone started following him as an animal. Little by little, as people walked, stories started to emerge. (The advantage of the 'Walking Show' was that while you were walking, you could think about what on earth you were going to do next!) In fact, all drama is based on the idea of two points of view: there is person A, and person B, who encounter each other and have some kind of relationship. Walking enabled us to explore these relationships. One person steps forward, the other retreats in response. One person walks, another follows. Just through these simple actions you can suggest that you are enemies, or lovers, or friends. Like the 'Bread Show' and the 'Shoe Show', the

'Walking Show' was based on a simple concept that was relevant anywhere in the world. It didn't need language. It was not linked to any cultural tradition. It was universal. We performed these stories many times during our journey.

In some communities we visited, the villagers gave us chickens as a token of their gratitude. In one place, we took the chickens to the next village as a gift. After the performance the Chief said, 'We ought to make a meal for you, but there isn't enough time. Please accept this sheep, to add something to your dinner.'

So we were stuck with this live sheep. Later, a huge argument broke out about what to do with the wretched animal. All the women were utterly against the eating of the sheep. Among the men some peculiar ideas emerged, such as 'Decorate the sheep with red paint and release her'. In the end, we thought 'When in Rome . . .' and decided to eat the sheep as the village chief had recommended.

The sheep was taken to a rocky place. Two of the men held its legs, and a French actor cut its throat. The red blood splashed onto the white fleece, and spattered onto a rock. I imagined that the ancient Western rites of sacrifice might have looked like this. I could not run away from the scene, since I had voted for the eating of the sheep. I stood there motionless, and watched the running blood. I remembered the blood flowing from me when I played the Syrian soldier in *Salome*. I remembered the death of Mishima. Then I knew I wanted my own death to be bloodless.

The sheep was skinned and the flesh appeared. The blood had flowed down the rock and dyed the ground red. Dinner time came and the mutton stew was ready. The women would not speak to us. First I put rice on my plate, and then poured the stew on top. I had to force myself to eat it. The image of the thin sheep, looking around bewildered, kept returning to me. I finished the worst meal of my life and went to bed. I woke up in the middle of the night with a sudden stomach pain and dashed for the field. I had diarrhoea like water. After that I dreamt about the sheep. However, the following morning I woke up feeling fine. The diarrhoea had already gone. The skin of the sheep travelled with us for the rest of the tour.

In most cases we camped outside villages, but sometimes we set up inside, in order to experience the atmosphere of the community, as a preparation for the following day's performance. On these occasions there was total chaos. Villagers came into our camp full of curiosity. Some offered their help, some just tried to start a conversation. We had no privacy at all. We couldn't even rest. In the end, the English guides surrounded the camp with a rope, since there were too many visitors and they were worried about possible thefts. The locals could not enter this enclosure, but they kept their eyes on every movement from outside the rope. They were surprised, amazed and amused. We were like monkeys in a zoo. It seemed that watching us was far more interesting and amusing than our shows. When our cook went to take the stale bread to the rubbish dump, all the villagers dashed after him to get some. Outside the Sahara itself, most villages had ample food, and the people were not really hungry. They wanted to taste the left-overs out of curiosity. They wanted to know what sort of stuff we ate. There were some clever ones who found various reasons for entering inside the rope enclosure. They enjoyed being the exceptions. This made me remember the time of the American occupation of post-war Japan.

When I was young some of my clever playmates got friendly with the American soldiers, and received chocolate and chewing gum from them. Sometimes they were allowed to enter the camp and they had a good time there. Of course, I wanted to join in. I wanted to have chocolate, but on the other hand I had too much pride. It seemed a humiliation to get what you want by playing up to someone. I don't know why, but somehow I looked down on the American army of occupation. I did not like their easygoing manner. I felt that the chocolate would not taste very good if I had to get it by playing up to such frivolous people. I then reasoned, 'Since I don't want anything from them, I'm better off keeping my distance.' And so I persuaded myself not to get too close to the metal mesh fence of the camp.

Now, in Africa, I found myself on the receiving end, and I disliked it. The people gathered round the rope might be the same sort as my clever schoolfriends, or perhaps even prostitutes. Probably inside those villages there were people who genuinely wanted to get to know us, but their pride prevented them approaching us, just as my own pride had stopped me approaching the American soldiers. And these more reserved villagers may have been the kind of people we really wanted to meet.

And what about me? We called our group 'international', but in fact most of the people were white. The only exceptions were myself and Malick Bagayogo, an actor from Mali. Since, in certain areas, he tended to behave in the same way as a white person, he was regarded as a sort of 'special' African. I felt guilty about being inside the rope. It is quite likely that I was behaving in the same way as that African actor. In South Africa, or the USA, where strong racial prejudice exists, Japanese are always treated as 'white'. Japanese tend to accept this as a matter of course. They have learned the 'white' culture very well. They imitate Western food, their clothes, things to see, things to listen to, everything under the sun. I also take advantage of the situation. But the reality is different. In the minds of white people, the Japanese are definitely a separate race. Of course, that is the literal truth. But sometimes we Japanese have peculiar ideas. Probably we would like to imagine that we are a kind of honorary 'white'. But Westerners and Japanese people are very different from each other. The Japanese language, the way of thinking, the world-view, and so on, have all been shaped by a particular history. In the same way, Western culture reflects its historical origins in Europe. The difference between these two traditions is profound.

For this reason, I could not stand the sight of myself in that African village, comfortably sitting inside the rope, behaving as if I were one of the whites. I thought perhaps I should place myself on the rope like a tightrope walker, or even put myself outside the rope, and observe what was going on inside.

The Western rational, scientific point of view, exemplified by Descartes' saying, 'Cogito ergo sum' ('I think, therefore I am'), can create a limited vision of reality. It is logical, but it is insufficient. We need to find another, deeper level of communication. One that is not based on sharing Western concepts and philosophies. In ancient Greece, theatre was the expression of the union between the individual and the Divine. People who ordinarily lived separate lives came together temporarily in the theatre, where they experienced a sense of unification with each other, the world, and their gods.

Nowadays, people have lost the sense of being members of an integrated community with a shared sense of the sacred. Some people are atheists, some are existentialists, some follow a particular religion. Our belief system has become splintered, and it is difficult to find common ground with other people. So it is impossible to perform the kind of theatre that existed in ancient Greece. Nonetheless it is still worthwhile attempting to create a theatre that unifies people as much as possible.

But if you restrict yourself to communicating on the level of concepts based on European logical philosophy, you cannot go beyond a Western audience. That requires something more.

Within all cultures there is some sense of the sacred. To create theatre that goes beyond any particular culture, the actor must spin an invisible thread between his own sense of the sacred and that of the audience. He must also attempt to link the members of the audience with each other on this level. This was a part of what the group was trying to do through its research and explorations. Sometimes we achieved it, sometimes we didn't.

Occasionally, we ended up penned behind a rope barrier, totally isolated from our audience.

Travelling south we left the Islamic world behind, and the religions became polytheistic, based on the worship of nature and spirits. In fact, these religions are very similar to Japanese Shintoism. As in Shintoism, there is no religious founder, no dogma, and the object of worship can be anything, a carved phallus or a large tree in the centre of the village. In this kind of pantheistic religion everything is sacred.

We went to Nigeria, to a small town called Oshogbo which has a long cultural history. An Austrian woman had lived there with the local priestesses for over twenty years. Her name was Suzanne Wenger, and she was over sixty years old. When I told her I had studied Noh theatre, she immediately suggested putting on an Afro-Japanese dance as an offering to the shrine in her house. Since I had had the experience of performing Noh at the Kasuga-Taisho shrine in Nara (this is a famous shrine where sacred performances of Noh are offered to the gods), I agreed to the plan. Brook and I decided to visit her. On the way to her house, we passed a phallus, enshrined in the middle of a dirty ditch. Brook said, 'In Europe, we place the holy image in a spot that has already been cleaned and tidied up, and then we make it sacred. Here people have a more relaxed attitude. Everywhere is sacred to God. God is not something special.'

I remember that my mother used to say, 'Don't do that! The god of the broom-stick will be cross and punish you!' when I once trod on a broomstick. According to traditional Japanese beliefs, every single thing in the world has a resident spirit.

The shrine in Suzanne's house looked like a stonemason's shop. There were stones lying everywhere on the ground. Some were square, some were round, and some were phallus-shaped. We couldn't work out where the actual altar was. In fact, the whole room was the altar! I was permitted to enter the room but Brook wasn't. He had to watch the dance through the window.

There were already some priests waiting for us when we arrived. They were there to play the drums and to offer their own dances to the god. At the Kasuga shrine, and also in Esoteric Buddhism, the sacred dances and music can only be performed by priests, priestesses, or monks. Here in Africa the same rule was observed. Suzanne said to me, 'Initially, the drums will start, and then the priests will dance. When they are finished, I will give you a cue to begin. Will you dance with the drums?'

The drummers started to play. It was a very forceful sound, and had a completely different quality to the drums played for tourists. It was a sound to shake the very interior of our bones. I felt as if I were being taken away from this world, and being brought into a mysterious state of mind. The sound pulsated, as if inviting the god to descend to the shrine. Then one of the priests started to dance, or rather to move. The movements were simple, merely shifting the shoulders up and down, or front to back, while the feet only moved forward and backwards. As far as technique was concerned, a black dancer on Broadway had far more skill than the priest. But the priest's movements were outside the category of skilful or unskilful. He did not generate the normal sense of pleasure experienced when watching a dance, but instead possessed a core of force and energy which directly confronted us. It appeared as if the god was using the physical body of the priest to dance, or that the priest had been transformed into the god. The tension continued to mount and eventually the priest withdrew to the side, as if he was disappearing. It seemed as if my turn had come while I was watching, spellbound.

I wondered what on earth I could perform here. Among Kyogen's Ko-mai (short dances) there are a couple which depict a lucky god, so I could have danced one of those. But I am not a professional Noh performer, nor did I want to live in the modern day, while remaining deeply buried in traditional art. I wished to use this rare opportunity to discover something new that could emerge out of my traditional art. But how was I to dance? How could I improvise to that awe-inspiring sound of drums, and in front of the priests? Somehow I had to find a way to start.

I stepped out into the space, into the middle of the shrine, where, until a moment ago, the priest had been dancing. Suddenly, I thought about the life of a human being. We spring from our mother's womb, just like plants spring out of the earth. Plants receive energy from the earth and sun. Perhaps our human life is the same. I started to move slowly as if emerging from the earth, and then started to stamp on the dirt floor of the shrine. Then the powerful sound of the drums started to move my body. Normally we move to the rhythm of drums, but in this case the rhythm of the drums started to move me. Subjectivity and objectivity were reversed. My subjectivity vanished into the object and was turned upside down. My body continued to move.

Living may be like that. It is not 'me' who is living, but something, like the sound of those drums, which is making me live. I don't know how long I danced. I had no sense of time. It might have been ten minutes or twenty. There was a natural ending point to the movement. I came to a halt. I felt as if I were about to collapse on my feet. Suzanne and the other priests told me that I had managed to become the god. If that statement was not a mere compliment, and if they really thought I had achieved that state, then what was it that they had seen in me while dancing? I really wanted to know!

When we left the shrine, and relaxed in the priestess's room, the damp equatorial heat of this part of the world reminded me of our normal existence, where we spend our lives day after day. I know that a part of the contentment I felt at that moment came from the 'task' of emptying a jug of freshly made palm wine!

There is an old town in Benin called Abomey, which used to be governed by a king. Nowadays the king's power is purely symbolic, like the Japanese emperor's. Only the palace and the family name was left to him. We arrived in the town one day before his hundred and thirtieth birthday. Inside the palace, rehearsals for the ceremony were taking place. The king, who was actually about thirty years younger than his stated age, joined the rehearsals. He entered with several queens behind him while the ladies of the court danced and sang his praises. We were given permission to observe the rehearsals. In return, we decided to dance in front of the king to show our gratitude. Each of the actors demonstrated a movement to show respect to the King while holding a stick, as the Africans do. After this we hesitantly asked the King to dance. To our surprise he stood up straight with a smile and started to move with wobbly steps. It was only a slight movement. But when the King moved only slightly, the air round him was strongly stirred. His dance, with its subtle movements, was far more dynamic than the dance of the younger people. Normally we say, 'The large contains the small', but in this case 'The small contained the large'. Human beings possess this marvellous ability to suggest inner vastness through minimal movement, and this ability seems limited to humans alone. Other animals do not possess it.

An eighty-year-old American dance teacher once said to me, 'An African's movement is "rubber", Japanese are "tree", while the Indians are "water".'

'How about Europeans?' I asked.

'You can't really describe it as "movement"!'

Putting aside the question of whether he was right or wrong, the movements of Japanese and Africans certainly differ from each other. That is why I had believed that the cultures of Japan and Africa were totally different. However, when I was actually in Africa, I was forced to change my view completely. African emotions were exactly the same as Japanese, and I could generally tell straight away what people were thinking. After I had been in Africa for a while, I started not to notice the colour of their skin. Their faces seemed just like the faces of Japanese farmers. Even the character types were the same. The houses are also built in the same style as old-fashioned Japanese farm houses. While I was in black Africa, I fell into the illusion of imagining that I was actually in Japan. After all, I feel farthest from Japan when I'm living in Europe.

Looking back on my life, I had a Western-style education, I ate bread and drank milk for breakfast, and read mainly European and American novels. In spite of all this, I still don't know anything about the West. I have no idea what goes on in the Western mind! In the end, I became convinced that the place which is most remote from Japan was Europe, not Africa or India.

One hundred days in Africa was a long time. Spending twenty-four hours a day in the company of twenty-odd people of different nationalities was not particularly easy. There were quarrels, love affairs, jubilation and despair. There were unexpected 'happenings'. On one occasion an actor called Bruce Myers went mountain climbing on his own and got lost. Everybody went frantically searching for him on this rocky mountain, yelling and calling his name. Eventually he returned, having finished his climb. There came a point when I was so fed up with the others that I woke in the middle of the night and just lay there counting the days till the end. By the time we were back in the Sahara desert on the return journey, everybody was absolutely desperate for a bit of solitude. At lunch time, after emptying the tin of sardines onto our plates, we all walked off in different directions to find a little privacy. However, without hills or bushes, this was rather difficult to achieve.

During this period of research into 'rough theatre', I felt that I started to become a 'rough actor'. In my first year with the CIRT, I was still more or less working as a traditional actor. I never felt comfortable suddenly jumping into a performance with the audience standing all round me. I needed to hide myself away before entering the stage, and I believed that there ought

99

to be something 'mysterious' about an actor. Peter said that this was true in periods and cultures where there was a strong belief in the power of divine beings. In those situations, the actor, when he was performing, was not perceived as an ordinary human being. Instead, he was possessed by a god and was acting as its representative. Under these circumstances, the stage itself was a sacred area, separated from daily life. But today this sacred element no longer exists, and the actor is just the same as anybody else. Peter said that, for this reason, theatrical action should happen on the same level as the audience, not raised up and separate, as on a stage. The actor is just another member of the crowd until he or she steps forward and does something. Then they become an actor.

In Kathakali (Indian sacred theatre), the actor takes six hours to put on his make-up. During that time, he slowly enters another state of consciousness in readiness for his performance. In Japan, I used to do something similar; but in Africa, there was no dressing room, no stage, no curtain. Just the carpet on the ground. The actors sat near the carpet, among the audience, then stepped onto the carpet and did something. I had to throw away my old habits. I couldn't prepare my illusion before entering; I had to create it as I went along. There could be no preparation at all.

Eventually, by working this way, I managed to develop some confidence in my ability to contact an audience, even where there was no common language. Ever since then, even when working on a stage in Europe, I haven't needed a fixed idea of the play. I am at ease, simply responding. Now, if something untoward happens, I have the skill to deal with it. I have learnt to be a 'rough actor'.

One day, Peter asked a member of the African audience what they wanted to see. A man answered, 'We don't need comedy since we laugh a lot in our daily lives. We want something mysterious and fearful.'

100

He wanted something that was somehow higher than daily life. It suddenly reminded me of an experience I had as a small child. I was taken to see a piece of popular theatre performed in front of the local temple. I remember looking at the actors and thinking that they were 'special' people, mysterious and somehow frightening. I had totally forgotten this impression, until that man made his comment. These are very important elements, mystery and danger.

The desire for 'mysteriousness' is usually associated with 'holy' theatre. But even there, it is not enough. Unless it has a quality of danger, it becomes a religious ceremony, not a piece of theatre. Similarly with 'rough' theatre, there needs to be an edge of fear in the laughter. A sense of danger is essential to all theatre.

During our journey we kept returning to *The Conference of the Birds*, written by Farid Ud-Din Attar, a twelfth-century Persian mystic. The story describes an ancient time in the world of the birds when there was no order. Nothing but incessant quarrels and disputes. One day, a small bird, the Hoopoe, called a meeting. He said to the assembled birds, 'The reason for our constant arguments is that we have no king (god). Therefore let us go in search of one, and I will be your guide.'

The other birds agreed, and they set out on their journey. Many birds died in the desert of heat and thirst, while others abandoned their voyage and returned home since they could no longer endure the hardships. In the end, only thirteen birds reached the gate of the King's palace, after having traversed seven valleys. The Hoopoe told the guard at the gate that they had come to see the King. The guard replied 'There is no king.' All the birds were utterly dumbfounded. Some even fainted. They started to attack the Hoopoe, saying, 'If we had known that there was no king, we would never have come on this terrible journey!'

Even the Hoopoe was exhausted. All the birds then fell on the

101

ground in front of the gate and lay there to die of despair. Then the guard reappeared and said that they could enter and see the King. He opened the door, and the birds went inside. Each was handed a mirror.

'If you wish to meet the King, then look into the mirror.'

Each bird looked into the mirror, and saw a mystery. When he looked one way, he could only see himself. When he looked the other way, there was only the King/God.

Similarly for us, there was nothing at the end of our long and hot journey through Africa. All that you had left was yourself, who had journeyed for one hundred days through various places and experiences. There was nothing you could do except re-examine that self. In the end, there is only yourself, nothing else. This is the mystery.

6 Uniting the Two Theatres –
Conference of the Birds II

The third and final year of the CIRT's journey into theatre commenced. In Iran, we had concentrated on 'holy theatre', culminating in the performance of *Orghast* at Persepolis. 'Rough theatre' was the theme of the second year's work, and our researches had taken us to Africa. In the third year, we planned to unite these two theatres. For this, we went to America. We began our journey in California, and as we travelled across the country from west to east, we wanted to meet other groups who were exploring different kinds of theatre. At the same time, we planned to create and perform a new show, based on *The Conference of the Birds*. We had already done some preliminary work on this in Africa, and we wanted to develop it further. The tour would culminate in a public performance in Brooklyn, New York, which would show the results of the CIRT's three years of research.

The first stop on our journey was a small town called San Juan Bautista, which lies about forty kilometres from San Francisco. In the sixteenth century, the Spanish had constructed a monastery there, and the building was still standing. We had arranged an exchange with a young theatre company called El Teatro Campesino. The area was in the middle of an American wine-producing district, and there were a lot of vineyards. At harvest time, in early summer, many illegal immigrants arrived from

Mexico to work in the vineyards. Landowners took advantage of this situation and exploited the workers, paying them the absolute minimum and housing them in accommodation that was little more than a pig-sty. In 1964 there had been many strikes in the district. Their leader was a man called Cesar Chavez, and through his efforts an official union was organised. During the upheavals of 1964 and 1965, several young Mexicans formed a group to support and encourage the strikers. One of the central figures of this group was Luis Valdez. This group became the nucleus of the Teatro Campesino. As their work progressed, they retained their role of encouraging workers and strikers with music and skits, performing for them every summer.

They took stories from Mexican myths, and developed songs and dances. They performed in front of the general American public as well as for Mexican workers, and gradually became a well-established theatre company. We went there to collaborate with them on *The Conference of the Birds*, but things didn't work out as we anticipated. During that summer of 1973, a new wave of strikes broke out, and Teatro Campesino had to travel to support the workers. We went with them. Our destination was the strike centre further south in Santa Barbara.

On the way there, we stopped at a bar for some beer. Seeing that we were strangers, the bartender asked where we were going. We answered that we were going to the strike. His expression changed instantly, and he asked, 'Why on earth are you going there?'

It was just like the scene in a Dracula movie, where the Doctor announces his intention to visit the vampire's castle. The bartender turned pale, and wished us good luck with an amazed look on his face.

The reason for his fear and surprise was that the Mexican union was facing a dangerous situation. They were confronting another union called the Teamsters, which had the reputation of being connected to the Mafia. All the drivers of large trucks belonged to this union. The Teamsters were trying to get all the vineyard workers under their control, and were recruiting members of Chavez's union. The bartender told us that the Mexican workers were demonstrating against this poaching, and that if we went there, we might run into trouble. We might even be harmed.

'Harm? Us? How?' we asked in surprise.

'Well, firstly, be careful of dogs.'

'Dogs?'

'Yes, dogs. They may release well-trained dogs to attack you. But you mustn't blame the dogs!'

We looked at each other.

'Well then, we'll just have to keep the bus nearby at all times, so we can make a quick getaway if necessary.'

Just like in Iran.

But the situation had already worsened by the time we arrived. Early that morning, a car had approached the picket line at high speed, firing shots at the strikers. A Mexican worker had been killed, and the strikers were at fever pitch. They said that the men in the car must have been Mafia associates of the Teamsters. The attack only strengthened their allegiance to their own Mexican union.

However, for us the situation wasn't very good. What could we do in that tense atmosphere? Whatever skits we performed would seem like total fantasy, and we would appear complete idiots for attempting a normal performance in the middle of all this. At our wit's end, we asked them what they would like to see. They answered, 'The Teamsters'. We had never seen anyone from that union, but we imitated gangsters, just like the ones in children's comics. After that they wanted to see a 'Landlord'. So we stuffed lots of cloth under our shirts, to produce the old image of the stereotyped capitalist. If Karl Marx could have seen us, he would have burst out laughing. But even that cheap, stereotyped, proletarian-style theatre seemed some-how meaningful, when it was performed under conditions where a bullet from the opposing side was a real possibility.

The following words were spoken by Luis Valdez:

The reason we support strikes is not only political and economic. It goes deeper than that. There is also the issue of cultural humanity. In order to understand the moon, the Americans sent up a rocket and brought back stones from its surface. Do they expect to understand universal mysteries, such as the relationship between the moon and the sea, the relationship between the moon and women's periods by such a practice? Mexican culture, whose ancestors include the American Indians, does not try to understand the universe in such a superficial and materialist way. We are the same. We are doing theatre in order to understand humans and human society, and their relationship with sources of greater power, as embodied in the sun and the stars. Our support for strikes is not politically motivated. We refuse to accept that fact that the relationship between worker and employer is only dealt with on an economic basis. We want the relationship to be a more fundamental one, from one human being to another.

After the Second World War, science became the new god. It took over the role of fading Christianity. It appeared that science was an absolute system which could conquer poverty, destroy disease, end disputes, and bring peace. Now it is clear that this omnipotence was an illusion. But most non-Western cultures are still trying to catch up with Western scientific rationalism. People and governments all over the world are following this path, and discarding their own cultures and social systems. Occasionally among the people I met in non-Western countries were some like Luis Valdez: people who would not discard their own culture, but would try to face the modern world while retaining their own values. They seemed dazzling to me.

During our Californian stay, I had my fortieth birthday. It was a strangely quiet occasion since there were no strikes on the farms that day. It was a great shock for me. As it says in the Analects of Confucius, 'Man finds inspiration at thirty. At forty, do not waver.'

Suddenly I had reached that age, and looked around me. There I was, no house, no family, no savings, no fame. All I had was my body and my luggage. All I had gained were wrinkles and grey hairs. The things I had lost for ever were my old masters, relatives, and friends, who were no longer in this world. Plus my pure black hair and a couple of teeth.

Peter Brook was forty when he left the Royal Shakespeare Company to begin his new work. He left at the height of his fame. Grotowski also left the theatre, and went into the wilderness at about this age. As Dante says in *The Divine Comedy*, 'In the middle of my life, I found myself in the heart of a dark forest, diverted from the proper path. It is painful to describe the harshness and desolation of that stern forest. Even the memory of it makes me shiver. It was indescribably hard.'

I feel it is difficult for anyone to pass this mid-point of life. In Japan, we have a traditional belief that the age of forty-two is unfortunate for men, and that the year before and the one afterwards are also problematic. The unfortunate age for women is thirty-three.

In the evening of that day, I was strolling with Michele Collison, another member of the CIRT, in the ruins of the monastery in San Juan Bautista. Michele was a tall, well-built woman who seemed twice the size of me. As we were walking together, I felt like a fly buzzing about her.

'Michele, today I became forty. Walking with you like this, I feel that I have become smaller than I was yesterday.'

107

'Well then, I'll be forty in ten years' time. Will I also become smaller and slimmer then?'

A Swiss friend of mine who was a banker said to me, 'It's fine doing what you feel like, as long as you are young. But what will you do when you get old?'

'I'm happy as long as I can eat brown rice, miso soup, and tofu. Those don't cost very much, so I needn't worry.'

'What if you become ill? You may feel young, since Japanese people tend to look at least ten years younger than their actual age, but you are nearly forty!'

The people in the Teatro Campesino gave me a Mexican-style birthday party. There were colourful decorations, tequila, and the song 'Happy Birthday to You'. However, the lyrics were different to the normal version: 'Happy Morte [death] to You. Happy Morte to You, Happy Morte to Yoshi Oida, Happy Morte to You.'

'What! Happy Death to Yoshi Oida! What do they mean? Today is the celebration of having been born!' I felt as if they were mocking me. But in fact this is a part of the Mexican way of viewing reality. Being born is a happy event, and death is also happy. This attitude is not the same as the oriental belief in reincarnation. The Mexicans are Christians, but their religion is a combination of the Christianity brought by the Spaniards, and the beliefs of the native American Indians. In conventional Christianity people go to Heaven or Hell after death, but until the Day of Judgement, true happiness will not be obtained. Being born also means suffering. But for the Mexicans, both birth and death are 'beginnings', and are seen as being the same thing.

I had felt this in Africa as well. One evening, as it was getting dark, we were preparing for our beds on the outskirts of a village. The sound of drums reached our ears, and we wondered what could be going on so late in the day. It was the funeral of a villager. Since we were curious, we all headed for the village in

108

the dark, and after a long walk eventually arrived there. To our great surprise, the villagers were energetically dancing with happy expressions on their faces. They didn't take death to be a negative thing. It was seen as a happy event, and a cause for celebration. Remembering this, I felt happy about receiving 'Happy Morte to You' from the Mexican actors.

Before flying east to New York, we spent some time in Colorado, in the middle of the United States. There were many Indian settlements scattered across the region, and in some places you could find the serenity and beauty of bygone times when the Indians could live peacefully.

I remembered the American Western films I watched as a boy. Then I was excited to see the cowboy heroes killing Indians. Those heroes were wonderful! But in reality, the story was about the European invasion of the American continent, and the Indians had been fighting desperately to protect their land. They were terribly cruel films. In fact, John Wayne was a real 'bad guy'. But we saw him as the protector of justice.

It also reminded me of a cartoon I saw around the same time in my childhood. There were many scenes where some Japanese would cut off the heads of Chinese people, just as if they were cutting pumpkins. These cartoons also amused me, although a funny feeling would sometimes cross my mind. Now I wonder what happened to those Japanese cartoonists? Did they really believe what they were drawing? Did they really believe at that time that the Japanese invasion of China was just? Did they really think that it was all right to decapitate people, as long as they were Chinese?

We did some work with an American Indian theatre company. When we were with them, I noticed some similarities between their performing style and the Japanese approach. Their work was very delicate and sensitive, particularly in the area of voice and movement. It didn't have the 'toughness' that I often associate with Western theatre. On the other hand, Western theatre has a quality of 'unexpectedness', which becomes very evident in the improvisation process.

When I started working with Peter's company, I was surprised to see how many different approaches Western actors would use to explore a given theme. I was amazed at the range of responses. In general, Japanese people tend to be very logical and consistent in their approach to ideas. I can usually predict how a Japanese person will respond to a particular idea. They are 'rational' in their imagination, not unexpected or 'crazy' as Westerners can be. I could never predict how a Westerner would react to an idea; they would make these incredible leaps of imagination. For example, when we began working together at the CIRT, we did an improvisation based on a story, which was broken up into several scenes. The first scenes required the actors to continue moving upwards on some scaffolding. Then the final scene needed to be played back on the ground. The Western actors kept going further and further upwards as the piece progressed, and then they suddenly discovered that they had a problem. What would they do about the next scene? A long discussion followed, which I, as a 'typical' Japanese, found rather pointless. To me there was an obvious solution; if you need to be on the ground, don't go up so high beforehand. Stay lower down during the preceding scenes, and then you can easily get to the floor. But the discussion continued, until somebody said, 'Bring a ladder and put it against the scaffolding.'

This solution dealt with the problem, but also enabled the scale of the show to become visually bigger. The 'typical, logical Japanese' response would have reduced the scale of the performance. By thinking too far in advance, and by finding a 'solution' that avoided the problem (rather than solving it), the element of surprise and unexpectedness can be lost. In a certain sense, we need to be 'stupid'; logic can get in the way of surprise and unpredictability. Performing with non-Japanese people forced me to learn this style of 'creative jump'. It is the only way

110

to take the work far enough. It is one reason I continue working in Europe.

We left Colorado in late September, and eventually arrived at our final destination, New York. New York is the city of ambition. Everybody is frantic to get ahead, get promoted, to be a great success, whether in business, art, or politics. When you watch people walking in the street, you see that their heads are always ahead of their feet. They are determined to keep going forward. It seems that they perceive fame and wealth in front of their eyes all the time. Europeans make fun of Americans by saying, 'In conversation, the word "dollar" appears at least once every five minutes.'

But if Paris is cosmopolitan, New York is probably more so. People from all countries and races gather here with ambitions in every field of activity. It may be the only place where the Japanese are treated on relatively equal terms with members of white society.

During our journey across the USA, we performed our short scenes everywhere to local people, just as we did in Africa. When we arrived in New York, we decided to do several 'Carpet Shows' in Brooklyn. Our stages were in parks or community halls, and most of the audience were black. Their ancestors had been sent here as slaves from Africa. Therefore, they were the same ethnic race, but their reaction as an audience was quite different. As we had done in Africa, we sometimes asked a member of the audience to participate in the show. There is the same initial reaction everywhere in the world: the audience in this extraordinary situation becomes confused and doesn't know what to do. After that first moment, the reactions are different in each country. The blacks in Brooklyn reacted violently and destructively. Sometimes they swore and broke the props we used. That seemed to be the only reaction they could find. Once, a boiled egg was thrown. (I wondered why anybody was carrying a boiled egg!) When you compared them to the calm African blacks, you were forced to wonder what had caused them to change so much.

When you see the backs of people in Manhattan, you see loneliness, despair, and hopelessness. In Japan, the back view of a person in thought to give you a truer indication of their interior state than the front.

One day, the famous Polish director Jerzy Grotowski visited our studio in Brooklyn, together with his actors. At that time, we were the two pre-eminent groups in experimental theatre. There was a certain uneasiness in the atmosphere, since both groups were conscious of each other. Suddenly, Grotowski approached me as I was playing a flute. He said the word 'omae' ('you' in 'rough' Japanese). Perhaps he had learned the word when he visited Japan. But I did not realise that he was speaking Japanese, and without thinking, I replied with the sound of the flute 'peee'. Again he said 'omae' to me, and again I replied 'peee'. 'Omae' 'peee' 'omae' 'peee' 'omae' 'peee'. It may have lasted fifteen minutes. Then the natural finishing point appeared, and we stopped. We just looked at each other. We had often come across each other in the past, yet our conversation had never gone beyond 'How are you?' 'What are you doing now?' 'How long will you stay in Paris?' He seemed quite distant to me. However, after that 'omae' 'peee' conversation, I felt that I had understood his humanity for the first time, and in a completely different way from previously. True communication between humans occurs not only through physical contact, or conversations with words. It originates in a much deeper place. It can be described as the meeting of souls. Words may be needed, but they are only a trigger. For humans to be connected to each other by this invisible thread, we may need to use theatrical contact, as well as illogical communication like that of 'omae' 'peee'.

But for that, I don't need to be an actor. Concepts like 'Japanese acting technique', 'Japanese actors', or 'The international nature of acting', carry meaning only when theatre is viewed as an independent entity. If you take theatre to be a part of general life, those concepts become meaningless. You don't need to be a great actor, or to put on a fabulous performance, in order to impress an audience. You simply have to accept your responsibility as a member of human society. What is needed is that you yourself can communicate to others on a deeper level. Then how do you communicate with others? Liberate yourself? Another obvious question is, why on earth do I think that communication with others is so important? My preoccupation with this question may have its origins in my own character. I can only reveal myself on stage. In ordinary life, I do not communicate easily with other people. In short, perhaps I need acting as a sort of therapy, in order to liberate myself. But surely it would be wrong to choose a career in acting as a compensation for the unsatisfactory nature of daily life? How can a person who is unable to live his own life with contentment hope to move people? Only when you have found a certain equilibrium in accepting all the aspects of your daily life, can you hope to give a good performance. I prefer healthy arts to morbid ones.

We presented *The Conference of the Birds* in Brooklyn, in order to show some of what we had encountered in our three years of research. We performed for five nights. Each evening, a pair of actors would take the role of storytellers, and the other members of the group would act according to the directions of the leading pair. Every night, the storytellers changed, and the interpretation altered accordingly. There were five versions in all: Michele Collison/Yoshi Oida, Helen Mirren/Malick Bagayogo, Andreas Katsulas/Miriam Goldschmidt, Natasha Parry/Bruce Myers, and Lou Zeldis/François Marthouret. On the final day, at midnight, Peter and the composer Elisabeth Swados presented their interpretation.

These explorations eventually led to the full version of *The Conference of the Birds* in 1979. Later shows such as *Carmen*,

113

The Cherry Orchard, and *The Mahabharata* also sprang from this period of investigation. The fact that I became able to create my own productions, and other actors and directors who had been with us (Andrei Serban, Maurice Benichou, Miriam Goldschmidt, Alain Maratrat, Bruce Myers, Arby Ovanessian, for example) went on to produce good plays, also depended on the research. The impact of this period became visible as time went on.

At the end of September, we the 'birds' of the CIRT, who had travelled for three years to find the King, had to abandon our quest before even reaching the gate. We no longer had sponsors for the voyage. We split up, with many promises of eventual reunion.

7 Theatrical Research into Japanese Culture

After these three years of intense theatrical research which had taken me all over the world, I felt rather strange returning to Japan. I had changed, and while I felt the need to get back to my cultural roots, I wasn't sure if I could fit back into society. I was also surprised to see how much Japan had changed during my absence. Tokyo had altered enormously. The evidence of Japan's growing wealth was everywhere and many new buildings had sprung up. Japanese people were using Western-style computers, clothing and food, and fashions now followed the latest international trend. Japanese inner life and emotional attitudes had also changed. Unfortunately, Japanese people appeared to have forgotten some of the most interesting and elegant ideas that are a part of their tradition. One of these is the concept of 'Wabi'.

The word 'Wabi' contains the idea of 'poverty'. In terms of society's expectations, the things that are valuable are power, wealth, and success. But there are alternative sources of 'richness', which are beyond the ideas of wealth used in ordinary daily life. On the surface, a person may be extremely poor, living alone in a tiny hut. Yet that person may have great interior 'wealth', which comes from his or her sense of 'self', and their relationship to the universe. This is what 'Wabi' means: exterior poor, interior rich.

When you see the faces of people in the Japanese herd, everybody looks peaceful. In the West, it is different. Some people look as if they are on the verge of a nervous breakdown, others seem exhausted by poverty, while there are those who have the face of a predatory animal. Compared to these, the Japanese faces looked so happy. (Perhaps this is true; perhaps everyone in Japan is content; or maybe they are just better at presenting a cheerful face to the world.) Certainly, Japan has achieved great material success since the Second World War. But sometimes the Japanese forget that their good fortune is simply the consequence of their own efforts. Instead, they start to believe that their economic success is a mark of their innate superiority. This attitude is dangerous since it can lead to arrogance. Japanese society is now becoming very rich in material terms. I hope we can find a way to become equally wealthy in spirit, so that our interior is as rich as our exterior.

When I arrived back in Japan, I hadn't a clue what to do next in terms of theatre. I knew that I wanted to continue what I had already begun with Brook, so I decided to take advantage of being home by doing a three-month research project on Japanese Voice and Movement. In the previous three years with Brook, the group had spent three months of each year on research activities. I decided to continue the pattern in my own fourth year in Japan. Among the various things I had encountered in those three years, certain practices had particularly attracted me. These were the songs and dances of Sufi tradition, Tibetan Buddhism and African religious ceremonies. I was interested in the fact that these rituals were performed not for the entertainment of others, but mainly for the spiritual growth and transformation of the practitioner. For these people the songs and dances are a way of liberating themselves, or, as we call it in Japan, 'Gyoho' (spiritual discipline).

In Zen temples, Satori (enlightenment) is gained through the physical act of practising Za-Zen (seated meditation). In Shinto,

116

it is attained through Misogi (purification of the body and spirit through immersion in a river or the sea) and Chin-kon (pacification and deepening of the soul). Mikotonori ('Words of Praise') in Shinto, and Shomyo (chanted prayer) in Shingon Buddhism (a sect of esoteric Buddhism) are incantations which contain strong theatrical elements, but which are basically religious exercises for the performer. I wanted to see if I could also use my acting in the theatre as a means of spiritual discipline.

I went up to Mount Koya, which is the sacred mountain of Shingon Buddhism. I was daydreaming while listening to the sound of the temple gongs ringing out the old year. A Shingon priest called Hideyuki Nagaoka, who was an old school friend of mine, came along to see me. We had both belonged to the same high school theatre club, although he was my senior. After graduation, he considered the future and decided to spend his life as a priest in the Shingon Temple where his father was installed as Head Priest. He gave me a book on esoteric Buddhism.

Because the esoteric sects (Shingon and Tendai-shu) use more incantations, sounds, and sacred movements than other Buddhist traditions, they were perfectly suited to my research work. The Shingon mudras (movements) and mantras (chants) were unique, and the practice of 'Shin, Kou, Yi' was central to the practice of spiritual discipline. 'Shin' is the movement of the body, 'Kou' is utterance, and 'Yi' is will, intention and imagination (the mental focus). The unity of 'Shin, Kou, Yi' in Shingon is amazingly similar to the process of acting. When performing a role, the actor must transform his speech, his action and his thought.

I wanted to study these mantras and mudras, and to seek the state of unity where 'Shin', 'Kou' and 'Yi' are harmonised. In order to do this I had to undergo 'Shido kegyo', which is the training to become a full member of the priesthood in Shingon

117

Buddhism. In esoteric Buddhism, there are no books or manuals to follow, and the training used to take four years. Nowadays, some priests complete the training in one year, some do it in three months, while others may only spend forty days. The general aim is to train priests within a short period. In my case, the aim was not to become a priest, but to experience the context of practice. So I wanted the shortest period of training; a kind of 'instant Shido kegyo'. The training has to be given by an 'Ajari', a high-ranking priest responsible for the transmission of esoteric knowledge. It is personal transmission, from master to student, like water being poured from one hand to another. I had to find a master who would be willing to teach me. At the Shingon Shu Jiso Research Centre for esoteric Buddhism, I asked the late Aoki Yuko Daisojo if he would be responsible for my training. He was a very high-ranking priest, and was famous for his beautiful voice in chanting prayers. He was eighty-four years old when I requested his teaching, but he very kindly agreed to accept me. He did insist on one condition. I had to renounce the secular world, and shave my head. Shido kegyo is the training for the priesthood, and cannot be given to someone belonging to the secular world. It was a problem. Intellectually, I was convinced that there was a relationship between acting and a spiritual existence; 'God' (Macrocosmos) and Theatre (Microcosmos); Acting and Prayer. The three years of research activity had led me to this conviction. But as an individual, I did not believe in the presence of a universal energy, or a transcendent existence. I could understand the relationship of religion and theatre on a logical basis, but I didn't want to become a member of any particular religious group.

While I had experienced the presence of certain kinds of energy, and moments of transcendent clarity while participating in certain religious events, I was not at all ready to leave the secular world simply in order to pursue them. On the other hand, I was very curious about Shido kegyo, and its context and

118

methods. So I tried to talk myself into renouncing the world. After all, I was already half-way there, since I had no home and lived with only my luggage for company. And in any case, when the training was finished, I could ask to go back to the world. I decided to go ahead with it.

Since the Shido kegyo didn't start for two or three weeks, I decided to spend this time studying the movements of Yoga. On the advice of a friend who was a theatre director, I went to the International Paranormal Psychology Research Centre. My friend had pointed out that since the basic training practices of Shinto and Buddhism had their origin in Yoga, in order to research Japanese concepts it was necessary to learn about Yoga. He recommended that I talk to a man in Tokyo called Dr Motoyama. Motoyama's mother was a Guji (the highest rank of priestess) at the Tamamitsu Shrine, and was also a great shamaness, and Motoyama himself was a Doctor of Psychology from Tokyo University. He had also studied Yoga in India. He had established the International Paranormal Psychology Research Centre, and was its Director. The research was conducted on an international basis, and was linked with the work of the Swiss psychologist Jung. International conferences on research in the paranormal field were held there. It was a good place to start my own work.

The Research Centre was situated next door to the shrine of Dr Motoyama's mother. Here, religion and science had a 'Treaty of Friendship and Mutual Co-operation'. I met Dr Motoyama. He said, 'Our practice ['Gyo'] starts at six o'clock in the morning. You may find it difficult to get here at that time on public transport, but you can sleep on the floor in front of the altar in the shrine if you want. As for the practice itself, an American is already in the process of doing it, so please ask him about it.'

I then thought, 'An American? I have just come back from America, and I want to know about Japan. Why do I have to see an American? But that's what the Doctor told me to do, so I'd better do it.'

I reluctantly persuaded myself to see this American. This was my first encounter with the 'Hugh McCormick who no longer exists' to whom this book is dedicated. He was a quiet, intelligent-looking man, aged about thirty. Around that time in Asia, you often encountered a particular type of Westerner who practised Yoga and other spiritual disciplines. In addition, hippies were still about, and you could always see peculiar Americans all over the world. But this man was none of those. He was a totally normal American. He taught me slowly and simply the way to practise Yoga.

Since I was going to stay in the Tamamitsu shrine, I had to get some bedding, and so I went to downtown Tokyo to buy a sleeping bag. After sorting out my sleeping arrangements, Hugh and I went out to eat in a cheap restaurant. Since meat was prohibited during the practice, we had boiled tofu, miso soup, and cooked vegetables. He started to talk.

'I stopped eating meat so suddenly that my joints ache when I do practice . . . When I first arrived in Japan, I started to do Zen meditation at the Daitokuji temple. For two years, summer and winter, I walked through the city of Kyoto to the Daitokuji. One day, after two years, I had a special experience. While meditating, I decided that I would not move until the 'Truth' was revealed to me. I sat for a long, long time. Eventually, I saw a beautiful flower garden, full of glorious colours. I went on walking in it. I don't know how much time passed.'

He woke from that dream, and walked out of the Daitokuji temple. But for some reason his steps had become wobbly, and he could not walk in a straight line. Since then, he had been looking for someone who could cure this condition. In the end, he came to the Tamamitsu shrine, where he was finally healed.

Other than us, there were two American women living in the shrine. They had gone to India in search of a guru, but hadn't found anyone. They were told that there was a good Yoga teacher in Japan, so they came to see Dr Motoyama. They supported themselves by working in cabarets. In this employment, they could earn enough money to stay and continue their studies.

Dr Motoyama taught me many things.

'There are seven chakras in the human body. You can see them in Indian paintings. They are situated on the top of the head, the centre of the forehead, the throat, the chest, the navel, the lower belly, and the coccyx. They are a sort of special relay station for the nerves. They only exist while we are alive, and cannot be found in an autopsy. Normally, these chakras are quiescent, but through meditation, concentration or other causes, they can be woken up and begin to work. When one of the chakras opens, it starts to activate the others, and eventually this leads to the state that is called 'Satori' (enlightenment) in Zen. In that state, it is possible to perceive a circle of light, about one metre in diameter, encircling your body and spinning round. If you ask people whose chakras have been wakened to draw the light, everybody draws the same picture.'

This reminded me of a chapter from the *Divine Comedy* by Dante (Paradiso XXVIII).

I saw a point which radiated a light
So intense that the sight it blazed upon
Had to close because of the brilliance:

And the smallest star which can be seen from here
Would seem a moon, set beside that point
As one star is placed against another.

Perhaps as close as the halo seems to be
Around the light from which it takes its glow,
When the mist about it is at its thickest,

There was around the point a circle of fire
Which turned so rapidly that it would have beaten
The swiftest of the movements circling.

And this was surrounded by another,
And that by a third, and the third by a fourth,
And the fourth by a fifth, and then the fifth by a sixth.

After that came a seventh, which was so wide
That Juno's rainbow, when it is complete,
Would be too narrow to contain it.

And so the eighth and ninth; and each of them
Moved more slowly, according as it was
In order more distant from the first;

And that one burned with the clearest flame,
Which was least distant from the pure spark,
I think, because most in the truth of it.

My Lady, who saw that I was anxious
And in suspense, said to me: 'From that point
Heaven and the whole of nature depend.'
(Translated by C. H. Sisson, Pan 1981)

Had Dante discovered this state of mind, very similar to Satori,
through his own experience? Or did he get the information from
somewhere else? An interesting question. The other thing I
found interesting was that the image of divine power was
described in a similar way in both Europe and Asia. I felt that the
circular stained-glass windows found in Gothic churches, and the
Buddhist mandalas might also be representations of the same
thing. Dr Motoyama commented on the chakras in the following
way:

When a certain chakra is awake, you may hear voices from
somewhere, or be able to see future events. We call people

122

whose chakras are awake 'mediums' or 'enlightened persons'. The state of enlightenment is very closely connected to the spine. Once the Kundalini chakra, which is located behind the coccyx, is woken, spiritual energy will gush out and can cause a high temperature. If a person has Yoga training, he can control this energy and push it all the way up the spine to the top of the head. He can then send the energy downwards through the forehead, the throat, the navel, the lower belly and back to the coccyx, circulating the energy throughout the body.

In Taoist pictures, the Kundalini energy is depicted as a liquid coming from the coccyx, and being pushed up the spine, as if it were in a water mill. The energy is not pushed to the front of the body, as it is in sex, but is sent up the spine towards the head. Using the energy in this way can help a person prolong their life. That does not mean that you can live longer if you abstain from the sexual act. The important thing is to learn how to control the energy.

Dr Motoyama then showed me several photographs. Human hands were shown, with rays of pink or blue light streaming from the fingertips. He continued:

What do you do when you have a toothache or stomach ache? Don't you cover that part of your body with your hand? Subconsciously, we know that we can reduce the pain by this action. The Japanese word for 'treatment' ('Teate') literally means 'to touch with the hands'. These photographs were taken under special conditions using high voltage electricity. The photograph of the hand with blue rays was taken when the person was calm, the one with pink rays when the person was excited.

Every morning, Hugh and I got up at half-past five to clean the shrine. The actual practice started at six and was finished by nine. Then we had breakfast; cheese, bread, English tea. During breakfast, Hugh would tell me about the transformations he was experiencing inside. They were amazing to me. Sometimes surprising, sometimes admirable. In the end, I started to envy him for the interior life he was experiencing. It was the most enjoyable moment of our daily routine.

At last the time came for me to go to the Shingon temple. Hugh and the other people doing Yoga chanted 'Hannya Shinkyo' (the 'Heart' sutra) for thirty minutes as a farewell.

I arrived at the Shingon Shu Jiso Research Centre, which was part of the Entsu temple. The first thing I had to do was the ceremony of formal renunciation of the secular world. Before the ceremony, my hair, which was fashionably long at the time, was cut by a young priest. I saw many grey strands in the heap of hair that was piling up on a white sheet of paper. Since the clippers were dull, I ended up with an unevenly cropped head. The hair on the sides and the top were left to be shaved as a part of the ceremony. The senior priest gave me a Buddhist name, 'Shoko', which is an alternative way of saying my Japanese stage name, Katsuhiro. With that, I lost my family name, and consequently would be unable to be buried in the family graveyard. I wondered what would happen to my ashes. As part of the ceremony, a priest asked my response to the following commandments:

> Be merciful – do not kill
> Maintain justice – do not steal
> Maintain fidelity – be faithful

Since I didn't think it would be too difficult to keep them while I was out of the world, I answered 'Yes, I will keep it well' to each question. My hair, tinted with grey, was to be kept in one of the chapels within the temple. I felt sad, since I felt that my enjoyable secular life was also going to be kept there, together with my hair.

In the temple, I had to perform four esoteric rituals. In a sense, each one is like a piece of theatre. On the altar table, you place a cup with water, a flower, incense, and a musical instrument. Then you invite the 'god' to the table. This is done through three things. Firstly, you form mudras with the hands. (Mudras are specific hand postures which appear in Buddhist ritual and art.) In fact, with a mudra the whole body is involved, although the visible action only occurs in the fingers. It is a complete physical action. Then you intone a mantra (a rhythmic pattern of words) in Sanskrit. This employs the voice. And when you chant these words, you must also keep aware of the intention behind the mantra. This is the equivalent of the sub-text in theatre.

I had to do these three things at the same time in the presence of the invited 'guest', the 'god'. And through these actions I began to feel some kind of relationship with my 'visitor'. Onstage you do exactly the same thing. Through movement, speech, and intention you create a relationship with the audience. There is one significant difference: in the theatre you can 'cheat' an audience. You can sometimes get away with acting that does not engage your whole self. You cannot 'cheat' a god. In the temple, I performed my ritual in exactly the same way, three times a day. In a way, I was performing for the hardest audience of my life, even harder than when Peter watches me rehearsing. I didn't see these esoteric rituals as purely religious exercises. Instead, I was an actor performing in front of the toughest possible audience.

I spent forty days in the temple, forsaking the voices of the outside world. All communications, such as telephone and letters, were prohibited. All outings were forbidden. No alcoholic drink, no smoking, no meat. To chant the Shingon sutra

'Rishukyo' for the first time in my life was difficult and it took me a long time to get through it. Everything was new to me, and I took a while to adapt. Consequently I slowed down the three young priests who were going through the training at the same time. Because I was slow in everything I did, I had to get up at half-past four, earlier than anyone else. Cleaning toilets in the garden made me feel that I was truly in an ascetic training. They were not flush toilets, but the old-fashioned pits with maggots moving about at the bottom. That sight took me back to the rustic life of pre-modern Japan. It was February, the middle of winter. There was only one small charcoal brazier for heating. I had the opportunity of savouring the pain of chilblains for the first time in many years.

The actual practice was in the Indian style. The sacred words were all in Sanskrit. The rules of the ceremonies had all developed according to the lifestyle of the sub-continent. The procedures of the Goma (Buddhist fire ritual) were derived from the 'Ceremony of Fire' in Hinduism. It was only natural for such elements to be Indian in style since Buddhism originated in India. Somehow I had the misconception that Buddhism had originally come from China, so it was a strange discovery for me. Since Japan is an island country, clinging to the edge of the Asian mainland, most of Japan's cultural influences arrived via China. Even ideas such as Buddhism, that originated beyond China, passed through the filter of Chinese society, before arriving in Japan. Consequently, many Japanese are unclear about the geographical origins of various cultural borrowings.

The high priest, Aoki, was a truly great man. His followers told me that in his extensive library were many books on esoteric Buddhism. In every one of those books you would find thin red lines marking the text, following the tracks of the master's study. But the great man who had absorbed all this vast knowledge spoke only in very simple terms.

126

Human existence is truly wonderful, is it not? Look at this meal. If we refuse to eat it, it will decay. It will become mouldy and rotten. But if we do eat it, it will pass through our bodies and become rich fertiliser. Eating is not simply an act to extinguish our hunger. Through eating, food becomes excrement and returns to the soil. Then food can grow again. Therefore eating enables us to be a part of the universal chain.

Prior to that conversation, I had always thought that the act of eating was somehow shameful. Now I realised that you eat not only to sustain your life, but to fulfil your role as part of the universal chain of life.

The priest often said to me, 'If you have a cold, don't try to fight it by taking medicine. You should try to become one with the atmosphere around you. If you can merge with the universe outside yourself, then the cold will disappear.'

His followers told me that when Master Aoki stroked the body of a person suffering great pain, and recited the Hannya Shinkyo sutra, the patient would relax and go peacefully to sleep. Indeed, Aoki described this phenomenon in very similar terms to Dr Motoyama: 'From the human hand, there emanates something very generous. When you visit a friend who is suffering some illness, the best thing you can do is rub the diseased part without speaking too much. That is "Teate" (healing).'

He also said, ' I have no complaints, even if I have to leave the world now. I am so grateful to have been permitted to live for eighty-five years. In fact, my body has been damaged by accidents and other causes. It is a real wonder that I have survived this long. Each day I enquire with interest how long this damaged body can survive.'

Several years later, I had the honour of seeing the old priest again. He had not changed, and was looking well. He said, 'My old wife [priests in the Shingon sect are permitted to marry] has trouble with her legs and is no longer able to walk. I am caring for her, cleaning her body, and removing her bedpan. I am truly grateful for this. If I fell ill, we would both have to be cared for by someone else. Because I am healthy, I have been granted the chance to look after my old girl. I am truly grateful to Buddha.'

This great master eventually passed away at the age of ninety-five. The last time I saw him, he had become forgetful and did not remember me.

'It is sorrowful to lose someone, but if you concentrate on the middle of your forehead, and remember the person, then that person will exist for you. You should imagine that he is only travelling somewhere, and not dead.'

Even though the priest Aoki said this, there are people whose bodies I want to touch again. I cannot accept death so easily, even though I am told that the physical body is merely a temporary abode, and an illusion. Nonetheless I continued my ascetic training.

Doing the training in the middle of winter was hard. I put a calendar on the wall, and crossed out each day. I was longing for the end. However, the weather turned warmer towards the end of February. One fine day, the sun shone warmly on my shaved head, and the heat slowly penetrated to my body. One morning, I found a plum blossom as I was hacking wood for the fire ritual. Its colour was a delicate pink; it was a truly beautiful flower. Normally, not being particularly poetic, I have very little interest in flowers. But at that moment, it looked so beautiful. It made me wonder why we humans bother to create art, when such a perfect thing already exists in nature. Art is 'artificial'. Artifice can never surpass this natural beauty, and people are probably happy enough with nature's beauty. Then why do I bother myself with art? The world backstage in theatre is full of slanders, back-stabbing, competition for honours, and ugly struggles for survival. Why do I have to persevere in that sort of life? In comparison, the temple is a beautiful place. I thought about living in this beautiful box called 'Buddhism', mixing with those who have pure hearts, and giving my life to Buddha. Here, I could spend a better life than if I stayed in the theatre. The excitement of the acting world started to fade away in front of my eyes. I decided to stay in the temple, and give up theatre.

Two and a half months of research on the theme of Japanese Voice and Movement had changed my attitude towards life enormously. I had stopped thinking about death and committing suicide. I had gathered enough courage to see my life through until its natural end, when my body disintegrates. My insecurities about old age disappeared. In fact, I had become interested in observing how my life would progress. This change just happened; there was no logical reason for it.

'What shall we do when we are forgotten, alone, without money in our old age?' some people say in a romantic sort of way. 'We can live like a hermit in the mountains, quietly with nature.' But how many of us truly believe that this is possible? Yet in those two and a half months, I had gained the confidence to truly believe in the possibility. That was the greatest fruit of the research. It was wonderful. Alone, without anything, I still felt certain that I could have a joyous life. Or so I felt during the training. (Of course, my perceptions have not entirely changed since then, but at that particular moment, I had absolute certainty.)

At last, the time came to do the fourth and final ritual of my training. We did the Goma fire ritual. I put small sticks of wood into a brazier, added pure oil, and lit the fire. Once alight, vigorous flames appeared in the centre of the brazier, which is called the 'Mouth of Buddha'. Grains are then thrown into the 'Mouth' as an offering. I watched the flames.

While staring into the fire, I remembered a scene from my past when I was about four years old. I was in my mother's arms watching a house that was on fire. I was worried. 'What would we do if the same thing happened to our house?' Suddenly, I felt

129

sad and started to cry. My mother did not understand this sudden outburst and asked me why I was crying. I felt ashamed about crying for such a strange reason, so I didn't answer her, but still kept crying. Nearly seven years later, an American plane dropped an incendiary bomb onto our house. At that moment, I cried with relief, since what I had feared actually came to pass. Our house was burning. Later my mother said, 'It was sad that our house burned down, but I feel good that all your childhood collection of rubbish has gone.'

Sitting in the Shingon temple, watching the flames from the 'Mouth of Buddha', I did not feel sad either. I felt good, as my mother had done years ago, because it seemed as if all the rubbish in my life was being burned away. I thought, 'Well, I really should go back to the secular world. I should begin theatre again. After all, I have been acting for the last twenty years. This is my life, and I should not try to change it now. While living as an actor, I should practise what I have learnt. Living in the everyday world is probably harder than living here in the temple. Despite this, I feel that my path lies in the outside world, and I should follow it.' This was the decision I came to while gazing into the flames.

By the end, I was glad that I had completed the 'Shido kegyo'. After the final ceremony, I returned to eating meat dishes.

As a part of my training, I had sworn to renounce the secular world. I felt very responsible for the decision I had made. The obligation to live in a certain way still remained, even though I had left the temple. When I returned to Japan one year later, I went back to the priest and said, 'It is a heavy burden for me to live up to my oath of renunciation. Please release me from my vow and permit me to return to normal life.'

Somehow he persuaded me to continue. 'Don't take it so seriously. Just leave things the way they are.'

Those were his words. He is no longer with us in the world, so there is nothing I can do to change the situation. He also said, at the time I finished the training, 'This training is for young men under the age of twenty. I thought that you would give up in the middle, since it is physically very hard for a man of forty. I congratulate you on completing it.'

After my forty days, I left the Entsu-ji temple and returned to the International Paranormal Psychology Centre. I told Dr Motoyama about the training, and then met up with Hugh. He welcomed me with a smile, and then we went to a café in Kichijoji. Since I hadn't uttered anything except sutras for forty days, I had a lot to talk about! At the end of a very long conversation, I cheerfully concluded, 'I have learned many things in the last three months in Japan. I wish to share my wonderful experiences with others through the medium of theatre.'

Hugh listened, with a smile on his face. I felt that nobody but him could understand my story. He was the only person I could really relate to. I felt extremely lucky to have encountered him.

It was springtime in the outside world. Cherry blossom was everywhere. Observing the tranquillity of Japan, Europe seemed very far away. I did not really feel like going abroad again.

I named those three months 'Theatrical Research into Japanese Culture', and felt happy that this period had proved so fruitful. I felt that it was a real continuation of the work I had commenced with Peter Brook. We had started with three months in Persia, in Africa, and the USA. I now wished to continue the research in the same way in China, South-East Asia, and eventually India, where many elements of Japanese culture originate. But for the time being, I wanted to go back to Paris to continue the work with Peter Brook. Now that the company had completed the research phase, the group, plus a few French actors, were going to apply what we had learned to acting. The base would remain in Paris. The name of the group was changed from the Centre International de Recherches

Théâtrales (CIRT) to the Centre International de Créations Théâtrales (CICT). Peter Brook, together with Micheline Rozan, found a theatre in Paris. Micheline Rozan brought an astounding administrative ability to all the needs and problems of the centre. I am sure that without her, it would never have been able to develop in the same way. Together, they enabled the work to continue.

8 The Ik and Global Angya

In the spring of 1974 I returned to France. Despite the feeling of cultural separation from Europe that I had experienced while I was living back in Japan, I soon readjusted to my life in Paris. Once more it became a familiar place, and friends welcomed me warmly. Driving along the illuminated banks of the Seine, I started to feel that Paris really was the most beautiful city in the world.

In terms of my own living arrangements, I now made a complete change. I decided to live alone in an apartment for the first time in my life. Up until then, I had always had somebody to look after me; my family to start with, then landladies, friends who put me up, or hotel workers. Now, at the age of forty, I started to do my own cleaning, washing, and cooking for myself.

It was far more difficult than I had imagined! Washing quickly piled up. And there were new worries about things like toilet paper, such as, 'When will it run out?'

Once I got up in the middle of the night to go to the toilet, and I stumbled over a glass table and broke it. My fingers were bleeding quite badly, but there was no one I could ask for help. All I could do was to bandage them tightly, all on my own.

Friends often came to visit, but they always went home. As soon as the door banged shut behind them. I felt my loneliness very painfully. When I lived in Japan, I didn't have this sense of

133

loneliness and alienation. Everyday life in Japan involves lots of contact with other people, and even at night, you can hear what is happening to your neighbours, since the walls of the houses are not designed to shut out noise. People prefer to live in close contact with each other. Even in the temple, I was always surrounded by other bodies; there was very little physical solitude. Wherever I went in Japan, I never felt lonely; probably because it seemed that all the people around me lived under the same roof. The roof called Japan. Yet when I am in Paris, I feel this loneliness, even in the centre of the city, just as much as if I were in the middle of the desert.

I remember a scene from a Jean-Paul Sartre play. In this scene the central character is walking down a street, when he realises that he shares no common ground with the rest of humanity, and that there is a sense of nothingness at the bottom of existence. In the same way, there is nothing I can share with the people I come across in the streets of Paris. Nobody seems to expect any real human exchange with others. Even when you are cheerfully chatting away to people, there is a kind of cold breeze blowing through the bottom of your heart. Sometimes it seems to me that I am also turning into one of these empty people. When I am alone, without any work engagement, the only thing I can rely on for communication is the telephone. Fortunately when a friend answers the telephone I have someone to talk to. Otherwise, the only solution would be to get a dog for the purpose of conversation. But I prefer the telephone. The calling tones for each country are different, and quite specific. When I hear a particular tone, I can say, 'Oh, the British sound' or 'Ah, the Japanese tone', and I feel quite sentimental and nostalgic.

Around this same time, I also began to discover a sense of sheer happiness in living my simple life. Once, when I was listening to music on the radio and eating brown rice and miso soup which I had cooked for myself, I felt tears of utter joy rise to my eyes. These new sensations were probably linked to my experiences in the temple, especially my changed attitude towards suicide. I was now content to continue living until my life came to its natural end. In fact, I was quite curious to see how it would all turn out.

In that autumn of 1974, we performed for the first time on a Parisian stage. Peter had found an old theatre called the Bouffes du Nord, just north of the Gare du Nord. The building had been damaged by fire about twenty years previously, and had been left closed since then. Peter decided to leave the theatre in its fire-gutted state, and even the part that was renovated was designed to blend in with the 'ruin'.

The company's first production at the Bouffes du Nord was Shakespeare's *Timon of Athens*, performed in French. It was also a return to the use of text written in a modern European language. The work we did in Iran used ancient languages, as well as created text, and in Africa we had to find means of communication that were not dependent on the use of words. In a sense, *Timon of Athens* was a return to normal Western-style theatre. We had a space, we had a text, we rehearsed, and we waited for our audience. We were no longer doing pure research; we were back in society.

Of the eleven birds who had left New York, seven came to Paris. Of these only two were French speakers. We needed to find another ten or so French actors for the production. Jean-Pierre Vincent, who had his own group, came to work as Brook's collaborator, and he suggested various people to Peter. Eventually we formed a new company for *Timon of Athens*.

The first task we had to undertake was the creation of a team spirit. During our research work we discovered that the sense of being a unified group had to exist. Otherwise the performances didn't work. So we had to concentrate on creating a single team, and especially connecting the new members of the group with those who had been involved with the work of the previous three years. We did a lot of improvisations to develop the awareness of the invisible thread that connects actors to each other.

Some of these improvisations were similar to the ones we had done in Iran and Africa. But there was one major difference. Now that all of the actors in *Timon of Athens* spoke French, we could use real speech in the improvisations. However, we soon discovered that by using speech, we lost our physicality and power. People just stood around talking at each other, without any real contact or exchange of energy. We had to find a way to recapture our energy, and physical directness. So Peter developed the 'Door Show'; a series of improvisations around a door positioned in the centre of the space. It could be open or closed; it could separate inside from outside; it could be the passage from one room to another. Through the 'Door' it was possible to explore many different situations. Sometimes it was a religious door, a passage to another world. Or it could be a domestic door, or even an abstract image. With this 'Door Show' (and other improvisations) we toured migrant hostels and schools, and in the process we established a new sense of unity. In addition, it was a non-verbal piece, and it demanded a very high level of physical energy.

The decision to employ language, and, in particular, a French translation of Shakespeare's text, proved valuable in other ways. When Shakespeare's plays were originally performed, the language had to be accessible, since his audience was drawn from all social classes. Artisans and peasants would watch, along with merchants and aristocrats. The modern audience for Shakespeare is largely middle class, partly because the text is so far removed from ordinary speech that it demands an 'educated' audience. Peter wanted to return to a style of Shakespearean performance that could have the same impact as the original sixteenth-century version. A French translation uses modern language, and so would be easily understood by everyone. Furthermore, over the intervening four hundred years since the.

text was written, many of the words had lost their energy and impact. Peter asked Jean-Claude Carriere, who was doing the translation, to ensure that the French text had the same kind of power as existed in the English original.

When Peter staged the play at the Bouffes du Nord, he used another important concept that we had discovered in Africa: the playing area had to be on the same physical level as the first row of the audience. In that way the audience could feel that the action was taking place in their midst. From there, the second row would be raised up, for reasons of visibility, and so on with each succeeding tier of seating. While it is important to be in the middle of the audience, we had also discovered in Africa that it is extremely difficult to perform to an audience which is all round you. Three sides is the maximum. So our space at the Bouffes du Nord became three-sided, with the front row of the audience on the same level as the actors. In this way, the audience is looking down on the action, rather than up to the stage. This makes an enormous difference to the relationship between the actors and the audience. In addition, there was no proscenium arch. The stage was not a separate world to that of the public. Everything happened in the middle of the audience. It was the same space, the same world. Here, something can be shared between the actors and the audience.

Prior to each performance, the group sits together in silence for five minutes. We had started this practice when we were in Africa, but what we do nowadays is slightly different. In Africa there was no aim or purpose behind the silence. Each person had to find their own reason for sitting there. But in Paris, we had a real purpose; to cut ourselves off from the problems of daily life, and to focus ourselves as a group on the coming performance. Sometimes we stay silent, or sometimes we may discuss some small technical point, such as: 'In that scene your hat always falls off. Do you want me to take it from you?'

This kind of discussion is also a preparation for the show. In mainstream Western theatre, the actors generally meet each other for the first time when they are onstage. They stay in their dressing rooms until they are called for their entrance. They have very little contact with other members of the company, and there is no practice of meeting as a group before every performance. As a consequence, the company loses the opportunity of renewing each time their sense of being a united team.

In this production of *Timon of Athens* I had a minor part. This was my first experience of speaking French onstage. Brook teased me by saying, 'You are the first Japanese actor to have performed Shakespeare in English in a London theatre. Now you will be the first Japanese actor to do Shakespeare in French in Paris.'

I had only a few lines, since I was playing the role of Cupid. I had told Brook that I was too old to play Cupid, but he reminded me that Cupid was as old as the world.

While we had been working on *Timon of Athens*, we had also begun preparing for our next major production. This was *The Ik*, which opened in January 1975. It was an adaptation of a piece of research on village life, written by the English anthropologist Colin Turnbull. He had accidentally come across the village during a research trip to the Sudan, although the village was located in northern Uganda. The Ik community was undergoing extreme change in all areas of its life and social relationships. The villagers had originally supported themselves by hunting, but recently their traditional territory had been made into a national park and hunting was banned. Since they had lost their traditional means of survival, the Government offered them fertile land in another area to cultivate as recompense. But the people would not leave their ancestral territory, or their sacred mountain, Morungole, which loomed over their village. The mountain was the symbol of their life and community. So the villagers began to cultivate their remaining land, with the help of government subsidies. However, they had little success in this

138

reduced territory, since the soil was poor. From an anthropological point of view, it normally takes centuries for a hunting society to become agriculturally based. It was impossible for the Ik to transform themselves overnight. Along with this economic and physical dislocation, they suffered extreme hunger and poverty. Their social relationships collapsed under these stresses. Children would snatch food from the mouths of old people. People would no longer gather together to eat, but instead each person would secretly consume whatever he or she had obtained. Even mothers would hide from their children and husbands, in order to eat without sharing their food. What we consider to be 'basic human relationships' (such as 'mother-love') vanished. All religious beliefs were lost. People became old at the age of thirty, and died before they reached forty.

The preparation for *The Ik* had three aspects. Firstly, we worked with Monika Pagneux from the LeCoq school in order to understand the human body, and to become more aware of it as actors. Usually, in theatre, movement is either purely natural-istic or completely stylised (like Noh or Kathakali). However, there is another possibility which lies between the two extremes: a physicality based on normal human movement, but more controlled and clear. This requires training. You can't copy any existing classical theatre form, nor can you just move naturalist-ically. Monika helped us discover how the body functions; the bones, the muscles and the joints, and we did a lot of work on the spine. This was the first time that we had worked in this way.

We also watched a documentary film on the Ik people, where we noticed that they had a very particular way of walking. It was light and very controlled. This was due to the fact that they were starving, and so they had to conserve their energy at all times. They walked slowly in order to economise their efforts. You have to use a lot of energy if you walk 'badly', so they walked in a light, relaxed way. Our work with Monika helped us to achieve this style of movement.

Our preparation also involved a completely new technique using photographs. Peter showed us photos of the Ik at particular moments in their daily lives – people eating, laughing, or just sitting. We looked at the image in the photo, and then we imitated the body position and the facial expression. We started from the outside, but little by little we tried to feel what the person in the photo had felt at that particular moment. If you don't attempt to get 'inside' the image, you can't really construct a good imitation. Equally, if you really imitate the outside image in detail, your body position will start to generate feelings inside. After you have achieved the connection between interior and exterior, you start to play the moment just before the photo was taken. What led you to that position? Then you start to develop the moments after the photo. What happens next? Simply imitating the image is static, there is no sense of time. With the 'before and after' you get the time dimension, which is essential for acting. The work we did on the photos also enabled us to achieve real transformation. We used no make-up, but people 'saw' us as African, despite our pale skins. One of the American actresses was quite big physically, yet she 'became' a thin, starved villager.

The third thing we worked on was text. We contacted Colin Turnbull and asked him to teach us a lot of Ik words. With these, we created phrases, and conversations with each other. Colin Turnbull's original book was adapted by Colin Higgins (who wrote the scenario for the film *Harold and Maude*) and Denis Cannan (Brook's collaborator on *US*). It was later translated into French by Jean-Claude Carriere. Peter asked the writers to think in terms of a film script when they were adapting the original book. Often, when writers turn a book into a play, they attempt to situate all the action in a single space. They think in terms of nineteenth-century drama, like Chekhov. By suggesting a film scenario, Peter opened up the possibility of short scenes which could shift about in time and space.

As Peter was working on *Timon of Athens* at the same time as *The Ik* was being prepared, the *Ik* team got together on their own, along with the assistant director, Yutaka Wada (who had studied the Stanislavski technique for many years in Russia), and started working on the original book. We improvised using our invented language, and eventually we had a collection of scenes which lasted eight hours. We showed everything to Brook and the writers, and they started to select and adapt the improvised material. Originally Peter wanted to use all eight hours, but in the end he condensed the material. However, it made him aware of the possibility of doing an extended piece of theatre, and he developed this idea in *The Mahabharata*.

In *The Ik*, I performed the role of the craftiest old man in the village. He was the 'bad guy' who steals food, and obtains tobacco by ingratiating himself with the visiting anthropologist. My lines were in French when speaking to the anthropologist, in 'Ik' when speaking to the other 'villagers'. As an actor, I found the play very difficult. It was performed as a document; we copied the actions and stances of the village people exactly, and tried to give a detailed and accurate impression of their daily lives. In my case, I was following the personality and physicality of a nasty man, in a very realistic way. Unlike most plays, such as Shakespeare, there were no dramatic climaxes. There was no moment where you could speak and show your heart to the audience. Since there was no exciting emotional peak, or release of feeling, there was no catharsis. Of course, actors like dramatic climaxes, and I found it quite frustrating to just concentrate on following this character for one and a half hours. I wasn't an actor playing out in a theatrical way the character of a nasty man; I 'lived' that man from moment to moment.

In the spring of the first year of *The Ik*, I went back to Japan in order to prepare and rehearse my own production, called *Japanese Liturgical Games*, which was scheduled to tour the

USA and Europe. As I mentioned earlier, the reason I entered the theatre world was to become a director, so this production was the realisation of a twenty-year-old dream. I had already arranged the venues in North America (Canada and the USA) and Europe (France and Holland), and each country had agreed to pay the production costs.

I realised that it was quite difficult to raise money for a production, and you must have tremendous skill to get this kind of sponsorship. In my case, the only way I could motivate myself to approach funding bodies was by considering the value of the work. Peter taught me that if the project was genuinely worthwhile and needed by society, then the sponsorship would inevitably materialise. From that moment I decided to think this way, I started noticing ways to coax or persuade people to give money. If you believe that you are doing work that is genuinely useful, you can approach people without feeling servile. If the money does not materialise, it means that the project you are doing does not correspond with a real need in that society, in which case you cannot feel personally resentful or aggrieved by the rejection.

Now I had to face the difficulty of selecting the actors. After the three years of working with Brook, especially after the African tour, I felt that true theatre can only exist when it touches a certain universal energy, transcending our ordinary daily existence and reaching a higher level. In order to perform in a production that fulfilled this requirement, I felt that the actors should have some acquaintance with spiritual matters. For example, the actors should be the sort of people who believe that we are not merely products of our ordinary daily existence, but that inside us all there is an invisible energy, and that this energy is both a part and a reflection of the vast universal energy. However, it was not easy to find such actors. There are plenty of actors who can talk about Brecht, Existentialism, or Proletarian Theatre, but there are very few who entertain the kind of weird ideas that interested me. I decided to seek Japanese actors who were not a part of the 'Western style' acting circle.

My first step was to re-evaluate the research work on voice and movement in Japanese culture that I had undertaken one year before. I started musing about how these patterns were connected to Japanese philosophy.

In Japan, there have always been strong links between religion, the arts, and the martial arts. These links exist not only on the level of philosophy and ideas, but also on the level of practice and technique. The religious exercises of Shinto and Buddhism (such as mudras, mantras, rituals of purification, and Zazen) are similar to the exercises used in the 'Way' of the martial arts. They all aim to seek the truth via the physical body rather than the intellect. This traditional emphasis on physical experience and attainment, rather than intellectual understanding, is very old.

I decided to select people who were based within this philosophical tradition. The participants I chose came from various disciplines, including Shintoism, Buddhism, martial arts and Noh theatre. Their ages were between thirty and forty. Over thirty, because by then a person usually has more than ten years' experience in their chosen discipline and is already a specialist. Under forty, because we needed a certain flexibility of attitude in order to share our work with people from alien fields. I felt that older people might have some problems in this regard. At least that was my attitude then.

On the surface, each of these disciplines differed from the others, but they were all searching for the same thing. All the participants were people who shared a belief in the existence of some kind of cosmic energy, greater than ordinary humanity.

After discussion, we decided to view our project as a kind of 'Angya' (ascetic training through travelling, or pilgrimage). We were aiming for a sort of 'Global Angya'. The aims of the tour were: to get to know each other and our different disciplines, to

143

enable local audiences to understand the performers' individual fields, and finally, to present a performance/ceremony which would embody what we wished to achieve.

In each location on the tour, we set up workshops, using the title 'Movement and Voice in Japanese Culture'. None of us were professors or critics, and so had little verbal dexterity. Neither were we skilled at languages. Rather than explaining Japanese culture through words, we asked the students to do exercises in voice or movement. We felt that through doing these exercises, the participants would be able to physically experience the nature of Japanese culture. We described the workshops in the following way:

> There are two distinguishable strands within the tradition of Japanese philosophy. One is derived from the martial arts, the other is to be found in the various religions. They are closely interconnected, and can be realised through specific physical acts. For example, the acts of sitting in Zen meditation, chanting mantras, or forming mudras with the hands, are all physical actions leading towards enlightenment, and they heighten the practitioners' ability to discern the actual nature of human reality. Similarly, in traditional Japanese martial arts, the apparent aim is to kill the enemy, but the ultimate goal of these martial techniques is to reach a higher level of existence where the concepts of life and death are transcended.

During the workshop, each day's training would be led by a different teacher; day one, by a Shinto priest, day two, by a Buddhist priest, and so on. Each system had its own philosophy and training methods, which we kept separate. Below, I have tried to outline some of the main ideas and exercises.

Shintoism is the original Japanese religion. It existed for centuries prior to the importation of Buddhism from China in the sixth century AD. It really shouldn't be described as a 'religion', since there is no founder, no scriptures, no dogma, and no god. Instead, there is a belief in a kind of universal energy, which is called 'Kami'. This energy is contacted through impressive natural phenomena, such as mountains, large trees, rocks, etc. The word 'Kami' is often translated as 'God' or 'Spirit', since the conduits of this energy, are also called 'Kami', but it is not 'God' in the western sense of the word. In the ceremonies, people ask 'Kami' to descend onto the rock (the sound 'oh' can be used for this purpose), and then they pray. Afterwards, the 'Kami' departs again.

Since there is no defined religious structure in Shintoism, there is no agreement about what it means. If you ask different priests 'What is Shintoism?' each of them will answer in a different way. This is quite normal. Nonetheless, there are two recognisable strands within Shinto. Originally, it was believed the inheritors of 'Kami' were the Emperor's family. This became 'Orthodox Shinto'. As the centuries progressed, many 'prophets' emerged, and they founded their own sects. This became known as 'Sect Shinto'. Within Shinto, there is a tradition of spiritual training, although the exercises vary from sect to sect. In the workshops, we used exercises from a number of different sects.

In Shintoism, the basic belief is that human beings are the same as 'Kami'. You are, by nature, part of the vast energy of the universe. When you are born, you are pure and totally unified with 'Kami'. But because life is difficult, your original purity becomes contaminated by negative energy. Your soul becomes covered in a sort of spiritual 'dust'. When you are sick, or have bad luck, or even kill someone, it is not because you are fundamentally evil, but because this 'dust' has polluted you. For this reason, the idea of purification is central to the spiritual exercises of Shinto.

The first spiritual exercise is Misogi ('Cleansing'). In this you cleanse your surroundings and your body. Normally the body cleansing involves going to the sea, a river, or a waterfall. You shouldn't go to a lake since the water is still. You need moving water. If you can't go to nature, you can do Misogi in a cold shower.

The second exercise is called Furutama (literally 'Shaking the Soul'). This involves strong physical movement. In some ways, I don't think that this is a religious exercise. As I travelled about with Peter, I discovered that each country has certain kinds of movement that they used for spiritual purposes. Africans move from the tailbone, and use undulations of the spine. In the Middle Eastern Dervish tradition, there are whirling patterns and also certain repeated movements of the head and the shoulder, which are accompanied by a 'hai, hai' sound. In Japan, we have similar exercises. When you do these kinds of movement, they generate a sense of heightened spirituality, and they often appear within the context of specific religions. But their original function may lie outside organised religious traditions.

A human being consists of a spirit (soul/inner energy), as well as a physical body. Since we can see our body, we worry about it and try to take care of it. We give it food, Vitamin C, protein, and not too much sugar. We are aware of its health. However, since we cannot see our spirit, we forget about it. It doesn't get fed. But the spirit needs nourishment, just as much as the body. Otherwise it gets lethargic and weak, and we are no longer fully 'awake' human beings. The movements I have mentioned above are exercises to feed and revitalise the spirit. They are not directly linked to any idea of 'god'. In ancient times, people needed to be fully alert on all levels. Otherwise, they might die. So these exercises prepared them for hunting, or to respond to their environment (e.g. movements which utilise the spine may have the effect of stimulating nervous reactions, since the spine is central to the operation of the nervous system. So the 'dances' of African hunters may fulfil a practical purpose in sharpening responses.) In early times, these movement patterns probably

146

existed independently of religion, but because they contained a spiritual element, religions incorporated them in their practice. Over the centuries, as technology developed, people stopped using these spiritual training exercises in their daily lives. Nowadays, you tend to find them within the context of a religion, since that is where they have been preserved. But they are probably much older. In any event, the 'Furutama' exercises of Shinto are of this type. They are strong physical movements, incorporating the use of specific sounds, that are designed to stimulate the spirit.

The third exercise is called 'Chin-kon' ('Pacifying and Deepening the soul'), which is a quiet journey into the interior. This involves meditation, and focusing on specific mental images. These three elements, purification, spiritual movements, and meditation, are the basis of Shinto training.

In Japan, there is no perceived contradiction between the main religions. Buddhism co-exists alongside Shintoism, and many Japanese people practise both religions simultaneously. Indeed, until the last century, the two were so closely intertwined that they often shared the same temple buildings, priesthood, and training systems. Within Buddhism itself, there are a number of sects, such as Zen, Rinzai, Amida etc. All stress the importance of understanding and clarifying your life in order to achieve 'enlightenment', either in this world or beyond.

In the workshop, we used exercises that came from the tradition of Shingon Buddhism, one of the esoteric sects, and we chose to concentrate mainly on breathing exercises.

There are three basic states of breathing; in, out, and held (when you stop the breath, just after breathing in or out). In daily living we use all three, including the held breath. When you sleep you just breathe in and out. When you are dead, there is only the stopped breath. But as we go about our ordinary daytime lives we use all of them. As actors, we need to be aware of all three. Sometimes, people say that an actor should be totally relaxed, but this is not accurate. If you are totally relaxed, you are asleep. There needs to be movement from state to state; this is what we do in daily life, and so it is what we need for the theatre.

The exercises involve using these three breath-states in different combinations. At first, you breathe in through the nose and out through the mouth. Then you breathe in through the mouth, and out through the nose. As you do this exercise, you observe your breathing, and note how the different combinations feel. The next exercise involves imagining that you are breathing in through your navel, and then out through the mouth. Finally, you imagine that the breath comes in through the navel, and then leaves the body via the pores in your skin. Each time you breathe in, you hold the breath for a moment before exhaling.

Next, you add sound images to the breathing patterns. For example, as you breathe in, you imagine the sound 'ah'. As you breathe out, you imagine the sound 'oom'. Or vice versa.

Then you add hand movements. In esoteric Buddhism, the fingers are miniature versions of the whole body. (There is a similar theory in acupuncture, where the tips of the fingers connect to specific internal organs.) So when you move the fingers, you are in a sense exercising the whole body.

Finally, you add the imagination, so that you have a real inner link to the actions of the hands and breath. For example, as your hand opens and closes, you visualise a flower opening and shutting its petals. As these breathing exercises develop, they involve more and more of the body and mind, until you are using three things at the same time: sound, movement and imagination.

Each workshop session would end with the students doing one hundred prostrations. They would go from standing, to kneeling, to lying on the floor on their stomachs, and then back to standing again. At first, each student would do them on their own. Then they would do them facing a partner. Eventually, we made a circle with everyone facing inwards. The students prostrated themselves towards the centre of the circle, which was also towards the other members of the group. In addition, the centre represented all the people in the world.

During the martial arts workshop, we didn't do the exercises in order to learn fight technique. Instead we wanted to discover where the fighter's energy comes from, and how it is used. It also trains people to respond directly to each other, since the martial arts are totally based on the idea of 'partnership'. You need someone else to work with. If there isn't anyone nearby, you cannot attack or defend. In this workshop we explored several ways to focus our energy.

One way is through the use of sound. If you do a strong action and release a sound at the same time, it becomes more powerful than if you do it in silence. (Many societies around the world use this principle in work or fighting.)

A second technique involves visualisation. If you are trying to hit someone, and you only focus on that person, then your action becomes very small. This is because the actual space between the two of you is quite restricted. It is better to imagine that when you strike, you are reaching to the horizon. By chance, the other person has come between you and the horizon, and so intercepts this powerful blow. Similarly, when you are using the sword, you imagine that you are cutting the sky, not just a piece of bamboo that happens to be in front of you.

Actors should maintain this wide imagination in all their work on the stage. In this way, even small gestures become imbued with vast power. Also, the relationships between characters become a symbol of a wider world, not merely a moment between two individuals. For example, when you perform Chekhov, the play seems like small incidents in daily life, but they should be able to represent the whole of existence.

Through training in the martial arts, you can learn your physical relationship to another person. You can also learn

149

about a deeper relationship between the inner energies of two people; a relationship that corresponds to the energy of the world itself.

In the Noh workshop, we concentrated on learning very basic actions: standing, sitting, and walking. Since Noh is a minimal, pared-down style of performance, these actions are reduced to a very simple form. Through learning the strict classical style, students can sense in their bodies what the essential actions involve. These actions are also linked to breathing. Students might walk forward breathing in, or breathing out, or with a held breath. Each of these has a different physical sensation, and from the outside people can see the difference. Although there is no big change in external activity, the inner shift is clearly visible to an audience.

We also explored an important concept called 'Iguse', which is movement through imagination. In Noh, theatrical communication is a combination of physical and imaginative expression. If you have a particular emotion, you try to perform it with the maximum physical expression. This is the first step. If you manage to achieve this, you then attempt to keep the emotion at the same level while reducing the physical action. This intensifies the expression. If you manage to do this, you once again reduce the physical action, while maintaining the inner 'movement'. Finally, if you are a very skilled performer, you may be able to reduce the visible physical movement to zero, while maintaining maximum emotional expression. This is 'Iguse'.

In the workshop, we also worked with the rhythms of 'Jo-Ha-Kyu'. We would do speeches or series of actions while maintaining this particular timing pattern.

In all these workshops, we concentrated on exercises that would be of direct value to performers, rather than focusing on what was strange or 'exotic' in each tradition.

The title of the ceremony/show was *Japanese Liturgical Games*. The actual performance was based on the *Bardo Thodol*

150

('The Tibetan book of the Dead'), which is a kind of Tibetan Bible. Tibetan priests chant this, almost whispering, on people's deathbeds. It is like a prayer, giving instructions to departing souls on how to continue their journey after death. According to the book, the released soul will travel for forty-nine days without a body. If the soul achieves enlightenment during that period, it will remain in the other world forever. If it fails to achieve enlightenment, it will have to return to the human state, and enter the body of a child within a mother's womb. Since those forty-nine days of journeying are so tremendous in their power, the soul forgets everything in its past, and reincarnates as a completely different person. Through its description of the experiences of the soul after death, the *Bardo Thodol* gives instruction on how to live in the real world here and now.

We used classical Japanese and text from various rituals in the play. These are almost incomprehensible for modern Japanese people. We made this choice since we wanted the play to be understood through the energy of the words and their musicality, not their literal meanings. Since we were performing in Western countries, the direct intelligibility of the text was limited, and so the communication had to be on another level.

When I left Paris I had asked Brook what was the most important thing in theatre directing. He had replied, 'patience'. During our rehearsal period I came to understand the reason for his choice of words. First of all, it is extremely difficult to accurately communicate your intentions to other people. People will receive your idea in their own individual ways within their particular mental framework, but will think nonetheless that they fully understand your intention. Very few people can simply accept an idea as it is, without preconceptions. In order to be understood, you have to repeat yourself endlessly.

In addition, you cannot change other people. To do so you have to take extreme measures, such as are found in ancient Spartan education or brainwashing. If you take that kind of step in theatre, then the production is no longer a co-operative creative endeavour. It becomes a kind of Fascist dictatorial enforcement. Of course, in traditional arts like Noh and Kabuki, actors must imitate past techniques without questioning them. In that world, to learn is to imitate. However, in my own work, I was attempting to progress through the past in order to discover the next step for the future. If a director forces the actors to follow his ideas, they become mere robots locked into old patterns. In order to discover something new, directors should wait until something ferments inside the actor, and then build up the play from there. If the director commands the actor, the actor will only feel a sense of obedience, and he will lose the passion to take the initiative. The director should wait until the actor is ready to act on his own initiative, but in the way that the director suggests. Then the actor will feel that his choice is his own discovery, and will act freely and without doubts. This freedom will inevitably become a source of energy for the whole production, enabling it to expand and become truly engaging on all levels.

The show started with all the members of the company walking on to the stage together. We wore simple white trousers, like the bottom half of judo costume, and nothing else. We each carried a bucket of water and some cloths. The first thing we did was to clean the floor of the stage, and then we washed our hands and rinsed our mouths with fresh water. Several people asked us why we cleaned the space. Since the show was called *Liturgical Games*, we included a part of the ritual of purification. Before going into a temple in Japan, or participating in a ceremony, we always cleanse our hands and mouth. Even in Noh theatre, we purify ourselves and the stage before performing, but the audience never sees this part of the tradition.

The play itself then began with the chanting of the Hannya Shingyo ('Heart sutra') as the main character approaches the moment of death. After he dies, he goes on a journey through

152

the afterlife, where he encounters various experiences, and then he is eventually reborn. I played the role of the dead man, while the other members of the company created his vision of the afterlife. They encouraged him to discard his illusory attachments to life, such as desire for money, emotional problems, desire for pleasure. At a certain point in the play, these performers started to put on the costume appropriate to their actual role in real life. The Buddhist priest dressed in his robes, the Shinto priest did the same, the martial arts masters put on the traditional outfits, and the Noh actor wore his dance costume. Instead of being a group of anonymous performers, they became distinct individuals, each representing their particular tradition.

Despite the fact that it took more than five minutes for the performers to get dressed, many people thought that this was one of the most interesting scenes. Western clothes are three-dimensional. They have volume, since the shape of the body is echoed in the shape of the garment. In contrast, Japanese clothes are two-dimensional. They are unstructured, and are stored folded and flat. It was interesting for the audience to watch a flat piece of cloth being transformed into a three-dimensional costume. Also, in modern life, you use buttons, zips, and Velcro to fasten clothes quickly and conveniently. In traditional Japanese costume, everything is wrapped and tied, often with very beautiful silk cords. It was also interesting to watch how the members of the group transformed themselves through costume. The man in white trousers disappeared, and a Buddhist priest emerged.

In terms of language, it was a similar experience to *Orghast*. Since we used archaic languages that no one could understand literally, communication occurred on the level of intention and energy. In a sense, the style we were using fitted into the general trend of theatrical exploration. During the 1970s, people were experimenting in many directions, particularly that of non-verbal communication. Artaud was fashionable, and many groups were exploring physical means of expression which were not dependent on intellectual understanding. Although *Japanese Liturgical Games* was successful at that time, I don't know if it would work today. Anyway, as Peter said, the life of any production is five years at most. After that it becomes dated.

At that time I suddenly had an urge to see Hugh McCormick, and I telephoned him. He was still at the International Paranormal Psychology Research Centre helping Dr Motoyama with foreign correspondence and organising overseas trips. We met in a Soba restaurant in Shibuya, and enjoyed our reunion while slurping noodles.

'What are you going to do?' I asked.

'Well, I haven't decided yet, but I am going to leave Japan,' he replied.

It seemed that he had undergone some kind of a deep experience, but was not quite sure what step to take next. Seeing the state he was in was just like seeing myself. Although I hadn't had any profound experience like his, we were alike in our uncertainty about what we should do. We both felt that we were walking alone in some vast desert without any clear direction to follow. It was such a pleasure to see him again. Yet seeing him sitting in front of me, I started to feel sorrow and sadness. I thought, 'Once he leaves Japan, we don't know when we will see each other. We may never have the opportunity to meet again.' He was the only person I could talk to so openly, about everything. And he alone could understand everything I said. I felt I could not bear the thought of him going away. I was feeling as sad as if I were leaving my sweetheart for ever. As it happened, that was my last meeting with Hugh McCormick, because 'Hugh McCormick' has ceased to exist. And I could not imagine the shock I would receive at our next reunion.

The tour of 'Global Angya' began in Vancouver, Canada, in September 1975. Before each performance we held our workshops, with each day's classes being led by a different teacher. The first show was planned to take place in a Japanese community hall, built by Japanese fishermen and their families who had emigrated to Canada before the Second World War. However, there was not a single person in the audience that evening. One of the respected village elders had died, and his funeral was being held that night. Naturally, all the local people had gone there. This elder, like the rest of the Japanese community, had been interned in a camp during the war, and had experienced considerable hardship. He was a member of the first generation to emigrate from Japan. We asked one of the company members who was a priest (Hideyuki Nagaoka), to hold a ceremony of commemoration for the old man's long journeying.

After that, all our shows in Montreal, Stratford (Canada), New York, Amsterdam, and Paris were received very well.

I asked Peter what he thought of the show. He said, 'When you pretended to be dead, you honestly expressed what you imagine it means to be lifeless. But when an actor plays himself honestly, like a document, there is no theatrical interest.'

When I played that nasty man in *The Ik*, the audience could enjoy the fact that they were seeing two different things. They were watching an actor called Yoshi Oida, playing a devious, grasping villain. It was interesting to watch, since the audience is always subconsciously aware of the two entities, the actor and the character, and enjoys seeing how they relate to each other. But if you play yourself, it can't lead anywhere. Nothing beyond your own experience is explored and given life, and it isn't very exciting for an audience.

In creating this show, I had achieved my dream of becoming the director of my own company. However, I became aware of various shortcomings in myself through this experience. I do not possess the quality of leadership necessary to hold a permanent company together. Nor do I have the financial acumen that is needed. More significantly, I lack the fighting spirit necessary

155

to overcome these difficulties. I am sure that every member of the company parted with some sense of dissatisfaction about the work. Perhaps only the bad memories remain while the good memories depart. Possibly, this feeling also comes from within my own personality. I talked about this with Brook.

'Well,' I said, 'I finally succeeded in fulfilling my dream at last, and I feel very satisfied. But another question occurs to me. Is this present moment of achievement the ultimate realisation of my goal? Or is it only the starting point? Through my first experience of directing I have learnt that I am unable to be the head of my own company. Nor am I suited to the role of director. I no longer have the energy to continue creative theatrical activities. Throughout your long experience of directing, how do you continue to find the energy for the next production?'

'The reason I have continued directing,' he replied, 'is curiosity. At the present moment, through this work, I have understood this much. How far can I go with the next one? I think that this sort of curiosity provides the energy to take up the next project . . . And we have to keep on working in order to eat.'

That answer sounded like total common sense.

The Conference of the Birds III – The Actor as Storyteller

When the tour finished, I realised that I would just have to keep on doing theatre! Since then, I have been wearing three different hats: those of director, actor, and leader of workshops in 'Movement and Voice'. After the 'Global Angya', I directed the following productions:

Ametsuchi ('Heaven and Earth') by Mutsuro Takahashi. The cast was made up of Japanese actors working within the Western tradition of theatre. It opened in June 1978, and then toured Europe, USA, and the Middle East.

Interrogations based on Zen koans and commentary, adapted and performed by myself, together with a musician. It opened in 1979, and has since toured throughout Europe, North America and Australia.

The Tibetan Book of the Dead based on the *Bardo Thodol*, adapted by Isabelle Famechon. The original cast included an Algerian actor, a Kenyan dancer, and a Japanese musician. It opened in 1982, then was further rearranged. The second version toured France, Italy, Germany, and England.

La Divina Commedia adapted from Dante. The cast consisted of Italian actors, and the play was performed in Rome and Milan.

Yamagoe ('Over the Mountain'), an adaptation of the
Noh play *Kayoi Komachi*. It was performed in winter 1983,
with German actors, and toured Germany, Austria,
Switzerland and Denmark.

The Tale of the Chameleon, an adaptation of a West
African folk tale. It opened in Italy in 1986, and has since
toured throughout Europe and Japan.

When I directed these shows, I based my approach on the idea
of 'invisible theatre'. This kind of theatre is essentially born
through the relationship between the actors and the audience.
Theatre which is merely a display case for props, costume and
lighting is not real theatre. In an ideal theatrical relationship, the
actors should not provide too much information. If they do, the
audience becomes passive, only waiting to receive what the
actors give them. Their participation in the theatrical relationship becomes negligible.

The theatre I am aiming for is one in which the audience can
create the story for themselves, based on the suggestions coming
from the actors. Everything should be planned to enable the
audience to develop the story, using their own imaginations. The
actors should give them the absolute minimum of information.
We should exercise restraint in the expression of details, and in
the use of sets, props and costumes. Otherwise, the audience will
not experience the 'empty space' in which to exercise their
imaginations. An audience should not be treated like a group of
tourists who wish to 'have a look'.

I believe the true purpose of theatre is beyond the world of
objects and material phenomena. To achieve this universal
level, the actors and the audience have to work co-operatively
together. In this kind of theatre, the actor's technique consists of
the ability to provoke the audience into participating in the
creative process. In addition, actors must have the ability to lead
the audience into another time and space, different to that of

ordinary daily existence. This is a special technique, separate to the accepted techniques of theatre, such as skilful acting or beautiful movements. Instead, we must aim at transcending the level of shortlived pleasure and superficial skills. Only then can the actors and the audience walk together on a path to another existence. The energy that the audience receives from such a 'true' act of theatre will remain with them and enrich their daily lives. Ideal acting is the expression of the metaphysical world through physical acts: ideal theatre is the creation of an invisible world through visual presentation. You don't necessarily realise how the actors have affected you; you only know that you have been changed. Several years ago, I had a wonderful experience that demonstrated this.

When I run the workshops on 'Movement and Voice in Japanese Culture' I try to bring different masters to Europe each time. For the first workshop, I invited a priest from an esoteric Buddhist sect, but for the second, I thought I'd try to arrange a visit from a Zen priest. I went to visit one of the great Zen masters who lived in a temple near Mount Fuji, to ask if he could release one of his disciples to come to Europe and teach.

I made an appointment for 7.00 p.m., and travelled on the bullet train from Tokyo to Mishima station. From there I took a taxi from the station to the gate of the temple. The driver explained that he couldn't go any further, and that I would have to walk the rest of the way. So I started to climb the hill. Eventually, I saw a small light which was the lodge at the entrance to the temple buildings. On my arrival, I was invited into the Tea Ceremony room, where I met this great Zen master. I explained to him my ideas about the workshop, and said that I would like to bring one of his young disciples to France. He listened to me, and said he would think about it. He then asked me if I would like some tea. This invitation made me remember an encounter between two Zen priests. They came from different monasteries, and in order to see which one had the deeper understanding, they made tea for each other. But this wasn't really relevant in my case, since I am certainly not any great master!

He made the tea, and a lot of bubbles appeared in the cup.

'Oh, look!' the master said. 'They are like stars! Please drink all these lovely stars!'

I looked at the tea. Normally, when you make tea from the special powdered tea used in the ceremony, the bubbles are quite small. But these were huge, like soap bubbles and coloured all shades of pink, green and purple! Nonetheless, I decided to go along with the priest and said, 'Yes, I am drinking stars.'

Then he said, 'Do you want to see the altar and its sacred art?'

Of course, I answered 'Yes', so he took an electric torch and showed me all the holy statues and objects in the altar area. There were three or four statues of Buddhist priests, each holding a golden ball in the palm of one hand. I asked what this sphere represented, and he replied, 'That is your spirit.'

I thought that this was a rather odd and artificial answer, but I didn't make any comment. I just smiled and nodded my head. I didn't laugh. Then he said, 'Let's go out and look at the Zen garden.'

He opened the gate and led me into a beautiful Zen garden, which was filled with the sound of a waterfall. Zen gardens are refined, elegant creations, where each rock, tree, and stretch of sand is specifically chosen and placed so as to suggest a universal meaning. Some of these gardens are very austere in their simplicity; others are more elaborate. All convey a sense of tranquil harmony. As I gazed at the garden, the master said, 'Look at this gorgeous scenery. It is very theatrical, more theatrical than a real theatre set.'

Once again, I politely agreed with his comment. Although it was already December, I noticed that the weather was quite mild. I asked him if winter was always as warm in this particular region.

160

'No,' he said. 'Today you are warm and so you feel that the world is warm.'

By this time I was having great difficulty keeping a straight face. But once again I politely agreed with him.

He then asked me how I had come to the temple, and I explained that I had taken a taxi. So he telephoned for a taxi, and said he would accompany me back to the main gate. He took a torch, and we started down the path. He said, 'Ah! How beautiful the stars are tonight!'

I agreed, and explained I sometimes liked to look at them. I was particularly thinking of the stars I had seen in the middle of the African desert. They had been enormous, like images in a planetarium. He then asked if I knew any Buddhist sutras, and I replied that I knew the Hannya Shingyo. He said, 'It isn't necessary to say the whole thing. "Nam Dai Sho Jo" will do.'

He then suggested that we chant these words together. He began in a loud voice, 'Nam Dai Sho Jo', and I followed him saying the same words. Suddenly, I felt tears rising to my eyes, and I had to make an effort to hold them back. Just as we reached the gate, the taxi arrived. I thanked the Zen master, got in the taxi, and departed.

At that moment I realised that I hadn't got an answer to my original request! I had come to organise a priest for the workshop, but I had left without getting any clear response. The master had teased me, telling me a lot of rubbish! I knew it was rubbish at the time, and that there was no hidden philosophical or spiritual meaning behind his words. But despite all this, the visit had deeply moved me. I don't recall how long I was there, maybe ten minutes, maybe twenty, maybe half an hour. But the person departing in the taxi was different to the one who had arrived. I had been changed by the visit. In fact, that priest was a truly great master, even though he appeared a complete charlatan. He never mentioned anything spiritual, instead he basically talked a load of nonsense. But I was affected all the same.

It is the same in theatre. When people leave the theatre, they should be different to when they arrived. In the old days, people went to church once a week in order to be spiritually cleansed. Nowadays this seldom occurs. But good theatre should fulfil a part of this function. Like a shower, it should cleanse people. That Zen master had given me what I needed, although I didn't realise it at the time. In the same way an actor should touch something basic in the audience, whether or not they are aware of what is happening. It doesn't matter if people think I am a good actor or not. My real aim is to cleanse and change them. I try to act well, in the same way as that Zen master.

At the beginning of 1979, Peter started work on the third version of *The Conference of the Birds*. The first version had been presented in New York, as the culmination of our journey in America. The second version came into existence while we were performing *The Ik* at the Bouffes du Nord. At midnight, after *The Ik* had finished, the seven actors who had journeyed through Africa stayed behind. We improvised scenes from the original book, using bird sounds and movements, while the text was being spoken by a French actor. This prepared us for work on the third version, which was based on a script written by Jean-Claude Carriere.

This production also introduced three new elements to the work of the group: puppets, multiple characters, and masks. Initially, when we improvised, we played as birds. But in a way, staying like that all the way through the play started to seem rather ridiculous, and we began looking for other ways of expressing the birds. We decided to create a sort of hand puppet which we could manipulate to suggest the different species: hoopoe, dove, falcon, peacock, etc. These were not conventional realistic puppets. Some were just a piece of fabric wound round the wrist, or a carved bird's head with a stick to suggest a wing. One used no artifice at all, just two fingers to create the head of a falcon. We didn't want literal imitation, just the minimum necessary to help the audience's imagination.

In the middle section of the play, there were a lot of stories involving many different characters. One reason we decided to use the mask was to make the changes between the characters clearer for the audience. Peter was particularly interested in the Balinese tradition of masked theatre, and so he invited a performer from Bali to join our company. In Bali, masked theatre is presented as part of a sacred ritual, based on the texts of Hinduism. It has existed for centuries, and both the masks and the performers themselves are highly sophisticated, yet retain their sense of mystery and theatrical power. Tapa Sudana came to Paris, and taught us how to use the Balinese mask. In the end, however, we only based part of our mask work on this technique, which involves turning into the character of the mask. We used it occasionally when playing certain character roles, but more commonly we employed the mask as a kind of puppet. This was closer to the use of highly detailed, realistic carved puppets that you see in the Bunraku theatre of Japan. We held the masks in our hands, which were wrapped in fabric, and we manipulated them to tell the story. At other times we would put the mask on our heads as a symbol, and then 'present' the character. Neither of these techniques used the oriental tradition of complete transformation via the mask. This meant we had two new ways of using the mask, as well as the normal technique of masked characterisation. We also used 'facial masks', where an actor would contort the muscles of the face into a fixed position, and then treat that expression as if it were a carved wooden shape.

The style of acting went through three stages in the show. At first the actors were the manipulators of the bird puppets. Then they transformed into the characters in the different stories, using masks in various ways. Finally, the actors became the birds themselves, and continued in this style until the end.

During rehearsals we worked a lot with our bodies to get the feeling of being birds. We had already done a lot of direct imitation over the years, and we continued this research. We often tried to transform the entire body into a particular bird form, but sometimes we would just work with one part: the head, or the foot, or the hand. The voice work also continued and developed the ideas we had played with in Africa. We explored bird sounds, bird conversations, bird theatre. While rehearsing, we came across a major question: 'What are the actors doing in the play?'

The actors had no clear role. They manipulated puppets, became characters, and turned into birds, but their underlying purpose was not clear. Normally, you play only one character, and your purpose, as an actor, is to bring that character to life. In *The Conference of the Birds*, we not only had several parts each, we were also working in a variety of styles. So we hadn't a clue who we were! One day, Brook said, 'Imagine there is a temple somewhere, and once a year the local people go to visit it. They approach the box which is kept in the temple. They open it, and find inside some masks, puppets, and pieces of fabric. They take them out, and use these objects to tell the story of the journey of the birds. The actors are those village storytellers.'

This was our role as actors: to be pure storytellers. This idea was retained for future productions, and was developed even further in *The Mahabharata*.

Although there are many stories contained within the larger epic of *The Conference of the Birds*, there is one that has always touched me very deeply.

One day some moths gathered together to discuss the strange phenomenon called 'fire'. They couldn't work out exactly what this mysterious thing was. Eventually, after a lot of debate, one moth went off to investigate 'fire' in person. He saw candlelight from a distance, and then returned to the group and described it to the others. But the wise moth, who was in charge of the meeting, said that the description wasn't clear enough, and so a second moth went to have a better look. He flew close to the candle; so close that he touched the edge of the flame. He returned with singed wings, and described the experience to waiting moths. The wise moth said that even this description wasn't clear enough. Finally, a third moth decided to see for himself. He flew close to the candle, and then fearlessly plunged into the heart of the flame. At that instant, he became one with 'fire'. The wise moth said, 'He has learned what he wanted to learn, but only he understands it.'

That story always touched me. To really understand something, rather than just staying on the surface, you must completely unify yourself with it.

10 The Mahabharata

One day, just at the end of summer 1984, I received a postcard from Hugh McCormick which said, 'Coming to Paris. Let's meet at the George V Hotel near the Champs Elysées.'

I dropped everything and dashed to the hotel. It was the first reunion since we had parted in Japan, nine years previously. The entrance to the hotel was very crowded, and I had to force my way into the lobby. There he was, standing and smiling at me. His forehead was painted white with a red mark between the eyebrows. Pieces of yellowish-red cloth were wound round the lower half of his body. In short, he had the appearance of a Hindu priest. Taken by surprise, I cried out, 'Hey! What happened, Hugh?'

'Oh, no. Hugh doesn't exist any more. My name is Ishwarananda.'

He had forsaken his past and become a Hindu priest, hence his name was no longer Hugh McCormick. The famous food company, McCormick's, was owned by his family. He had thrown away an enormous fortune to become a priest.

I thought, 'What a waste!' Then I remembered that I had also left the secular world behind. It had been ten years since I had taken my vows, but since I knew I would inherit very little from my father, it didn't make a great difference if I renounced the world or not. I had also been given a new name, 'Shoko', as part of my renunciation, and had abandoned my family name. However, I still worked with my old name 'Katsuhiro' or 'Yoshi'. I started to feel ashamed of myself in front of him. I asked, 'Why did you become a priest?'

It was a silly question, but Hugh, Ishwarananda rather, answered me kindly with a warm smile.

'I had achieved enlightenment before I met you, Yoshi, while I was at the Daitokuji temple. I had always liked going to temples and churches, even from the age of four or five. And I appreciated that I would never marry. I wanted to learn Sanskrit, and so "a certain person died".'

I did not want to be answered in that way. Everybody knows that unbearable agony, pain, and sadness of losing 'a certain person'. Even my closest friend, Hugh, no longer existed. The person in front of me was Swami Ishwarananda. To me, the swami seemed distant, and I felt somewhat ill at ease with him.

'But why Hinduism?'

'I felt that Mukutananda was the best guru for me. The sole purpose of gurus is to lead people to emancipation. A guru is both active and inactive, both near and far away. A guru exists outside everything, but also within everything. Gurus know that they are not born, and that they do not grow old. There is no beginning and no end. They know that they do not change. A guru exists for ever, emanating, undefiled, and is completely pure. The essence of a guru is knowledge. Knowledge of the supreme self. They are the highest of all Yogis, and the physicians who want to cure all the diseases in the world. One should aspire to the attainment of the supreme youth, to reach the state of aloneness, serene and without desires and attachments, under the influence of a guru.'

The methods of meditation in Yoga can be broadly divided into two techniques. The first is to meditate on an invisible abstract image, such as the 'centre of the universe' or 'Kami'. The second method is to reach the invisible world through a

167

guru. There are sects that say that meditation through a guru is easier and more effective. Zazen (used by the Soto sect in Japan), employs this method of meditation. Wansuis (monks in training) practise sitting and meditating under the guidance of their master until they attain enlightenment. In Hinduism, there is another ceremony which is the ancestor of the Goma fire ritual. As a part of this Hindu ceremony, a guru asks his followers sharp questions. These questions resemble the koans of the Rinzai sect of Buddhism, and the Mondo of the Shingon sect. All Zen and other esoteric Buddhist practices are ultimately derived from Hinduism.

Unfortunately, the great guru Mukutananda had passed away, and had appointed his successor in his will. An inauguration ceremony for the new guru was being held in Paris, and this is why Ishwaranda was in France. All the people crowding the hotel entrance had gathered for the inauguration ceremony, which was taking place in the reception room of the hotel. Over one thousand people had gathered, and I could hardly get through the entrance. Ishwarananda and I went to eat in a café near the hotel, and I explained my next job with Peter Brook which was beginning in the autumn.

'I feel a peculiar karma. The last time I spoke to you I was rehearsing *The Tibetan Book of the Dead*, which was the dramatisation of a Buddhist scripture. Nine years later, I am about to start rehearsing a play based on the Hindu scripture the *Mahabharata*, and I discover that you have become a Hindu priest. It seems as if I am chasing after you.'

The Hindu scripture, the *Mahabharata*, is a huge epic written in Sanskrit. *Maha* means 'Great', *bharata* is the 'family of Bharata'. So the title means 'The Story of the Great Bharata Family', which can be extended to mean 'The Story of the Great Human Family' (since the Bharata family was the originator of the human race). The story is over fifteen times longer than the Bible, and it tells a colossal tale.

There was a power struggle within a certain royal family. Brothers and cousins fought against each other, until a titanic war broke out. A mountain of corpses accumulated on the earth. The family was annihilated, except for one man, who was a baby in his mother's womb at the time of the war. From that one man, the human race regrew.

The story is very popular all over India. Everybody knows at least one part of the story.

The *Mahabharata* ends when the hero of the story visits heaven and hell, and realises that it is not only this world that is illusory: heaven and hell are also illusions. The ultimate goal of everything is 'Mu', the Void, Nothingness. Hence the epic I was working on illustrated the philosophies of Hinduism. The man who had become the swami Ishwarananda was having to learn the behaviour and mental attitudes of the heroes and heroines in the same book as part of his training. At our reunion this time, we were both very happy to discover that we were working on the same *Mahabharata*. And so we parted until the next time.

Peter Brook and the writer Jean-Claude Carriere spent ten years preparing for the dramatisation of the *Mahabharata*. They faced many problems with the script, casting, fund-raising, plus travelling to India.

Peter's assistant, Marie-Helene Estienne, travelled across the world to find actors and musicians for the project. Eventually she found them, and when the performers assembled, there were seventeen nationalities within the group. We planned ten months of rehearsal. We found ourselves in a similar situation as the one we experienced when we first began work at the Bouffes du Nord. We had a mixture of newcomers and longstanding company members, and we had people from different cultures and languages. Once again our priority was to create a sense of unity and teamwork, which we achieved through vocal and physical exercises. Physical exploration has always been very important in the work of Peter Brook's group, but in *The Mahabharata* it became particularly intense. It is the story of a war, and so everyone had to find a way to create the body of a warrior.

Actors do not normally learn the real techniques of fighting, so we had no sense of a fighter's physicality. To address this problem, we invited a teacher of kung fu to come and instruct us. In addition, one of our company members, Alain Maratrat, had gone to Hong Kong to study this art. We were interested in this particular martial art because it had originated in India, and we felt it could give us a basic feel for Indian combat. We tried to learn the movements and techniques, but most of us were around forty years of age, and our bodies had difficulty coping. We were too old to start learning this sort of thing. There were torn muscles, twisted knees and damaged ligaments.

Peter then invited a Frenchman who had studied Japanese archery for many years to join us. We learned the movements of this martial art, which weren't too difficult. More importantly, we learned the inner concentration and fighting spirit that went along with the movements. We could take this internal attitude, and find a way of expressing it in a theatrical form. The movements didn't need to be accurate copies of the real technique, and we could use this inner attitude in a variety of scenes, not only those where bows and arrows were used. We found that if you really understand the inner state which shapes the movement, then you can adapt the surface patterns. This was a lot easier than attempting to do an exact imitation of a kung fu fighter!

Nonetheless, we did use the exact movements of archery in one scene, where the two armies rained arrows on each other. We didn't use real bows or arrows; just two sticks which created the illusion of weaponry. We had studied the actual form correctly, and then we developed it into a theatrical expression.

Just as we had used the essence of the interior state to create a sense of the 'warrior's body', so we used the essence of the exterior action to create a visual equivalent.

As a part of the preparation for the rehearsals, Peter gave the actors a lot of background material. He gave us photos and paintings, and films. We went to India where we talked to gurus (their philosophy and way of thinking is based on *The Mahabharata*). We also spent ten days watching an Indian theatre company performing their version of *Mahabharata*. Peter gave us many elements to think about, but he never suggested how we should use them. He didn't indicate what we should take, or draw conclusions about what all this meant. He let the actors, musicians, and designer digest the material themselves, and discover what was significant on their own terms.

There was never any sense of what the play 'should' be like, or of moving towards a clearly defined goal. At the beginning of the ten months we didn't know what form the play would take. We explored the various scenes in the same way as in *The Ik*. We would take a story from the book, and play with it in order to see how it worked. Also, each scene would be improvised by several different groups of actors. We would then 'taste' each version to see what it offered, without having any preconceptions about how this work would be used in the final version. In fact, Jean-Claude Carriere had already written a script before the rehearsals began, but he was constantly reworking it. He sat in the rehearsal room and watched our improvisations. Every day he would change the text if there was a section of dialogue or a scene that didn't work. Even the structure of the play was decided quite late. Originally we thought about doing a six-hour version in two parts, but during rehearsals we tried out the three-part, nine-hour version and then decided to do that one.

The first two months the rehearsal period were spent building our sense of being a united team and exploring the text, and another month was taken up by our journey to India. Since

171

The Mahabharata lasted nine hours, this left little over two months of rehearsal time for each three-hour part. Ten months of rehearsal sounds like a long time, but when you really look at the amount of work, it wasn't that much.

Brook pointed out that all the characters were greater than human: gods or demi-gods. We could not act realistically, on a daily-life level. In Chekhov, you can imagine yourself in the situation of the character, but not in *The Mahabharata*. We just kept exploring until we found a way to express the character on a superhuman level.

The work of Ariane Mnouchkine of the Théâtre de Soleil is described similarly to Peter's. There is one key difference. She is interested in telling a story while exploring a definite theatrical form. For example, she did *Richard II* using elements of Japanese Kabuki theatre. The company has also done work based on *commedia dell'arte*, and Kathakali. Obviously, she does not simply copy the movements of these styles, but the actors keep to the feeling of these classic forms in order to focus and unify their style of performance. In contrast, Peter avoids using specific theatrical styles. The company may explore something like Kathakali in order to deepen our understanding, but it is not directly applied on stage. Instead we try to find an essence on which we can build. In fact, there was no single method that we used to achieve our performances. We watched films, we read books, and experimented in many ways. We just kept going until one day Peter said, 'Yes, that's it. Keep it.'

As in *The Conference of the Birds*, we were a team of storytellers. (Indeed, Peter's main purpose in doing *The Mahabharata* was to tell the story in the West where it wasn't generally known.) He used the image of football to help us understand what he wanted. As if the play were a game of football, there were twenty-two team members and one ball, the ball being the story. Since we were all on the same team, it didn't matter who played which part, or if you changed characters in the middle.

Together we told one story, keeping one ball in play. In order to continue telling the story, you had to be ready to pick up the ball when your scenes arrived. Often, in theatre, you don't need to worry too much about what the other actors are doing in the scene before yours. But in *The Mahabharata*, we would stand and watch the action in order to see the best way to continue the story. Since the performances were never exactly the same every time, you had to see what atmosphere or feeling had been established before your entrance, and follow on from there. You would pick up the action and carry it forward.

This was similar to the way we approached the acting in *The Conference of the Birds*. In that production we were also storytellers, but in *The Mahabharata* the concept had become more complex. In *The Conference of the Birds* we had no defined roles or characters; we were constantly shifting from part to part throughout the play. *The Mahabharata* was more like a conventionally structured piece of theatre, and each actor had one major character to portray (although there were often secondary, minor roles as well). When playing your main part, you had to become that personality with your whole self, giving life to the character with energy and commitment. At the same time, you were also a storyteller, standing a little bit outside the events. In *The Mahabharata*, you had to perform on two different levels simultaneously. You were the character, and the storyteller; the character experiencing the events directly, and the storyteller manipulating the character like a puppet. In *The Conference of the Birds*, we only worked on the simple storyteller level. *The Mahabharata* was a more complex application of the idea, and more difficult to achieve.

Peter often returns to the example of Shakespeare as a model for theatre. Once he pointed out that within a single play you can find a number of styles of theatre, such as comedy, tragedy, or ceremonial pageant. In the same way, we used a variety of approaches within *The Mahabharata*. It commenced in the style

173

of 'rough theatre', much like the carpet shows we did in Africa. Then little by little we started to go into psychological drama, and also 'holy theatre'. Each actor had to understand more than one way of telling the story. Even within a character we would sometimes mix styles.

The play opened in July 1985. It was staged in a quarry near Avignon, as a part of the Festival. The whole production lasted nine hours – with intervals, ten and a half hours. It started at eight o'clock in the evening, at sunset, and finished the following morning around seven o'clock, after dawn. I played two roles; the first was Drona, Master of Martial Arts, and tutor to the princes. The second role was that of a lecherous minister who attempted to seduce the princess. We toured the world with this production. One year in French, one year in English. As a consequence I had the opportunity of appearing on a Japanese stage again, after my long absence. It had been eighteen years since my last show in Tokyo, when I received my farewell present from Mishima.

Before the company arrived in Japan, I had not been very keen about the idea of performing there. I thought that after eighteen years, people would be waiting with very high expectations. I couldn't stop thinking that people would laugh at me, saying 'What's that! He hasn't changed a bit!', unless I managed to perform better than I had before.

However, once the show started, I found myself surprisingly free from all these considerations. There was no special sensation, tension, or warm emotional feeling about performing in my own country. The audiences in New York are different to those in Paris. By the same token, the audiences in Japan are unlike those in other countries. Although I felt the excitement of receiving a different type of reaction from the audience of a new country, I did not feel that special tension and anxiety to do well in front of a 'home' public. Maybe Japan has become very far away for me.

Since the time I left Japan twenty years ago, I have lost the ambition to become an actor. The reason I have continued working as an actor in Brook's company was to observe the way he directs. Therefore I had to continue acting. When I was in the Bungaku-za, I tried very hard to be a good actor. But people all around me advised me not to continue, saying 'You do not have the talent for it'. However I continued, obstinately thinking that once I had begun, I would not give up. Even then, people kept saying that I was not cut out for it. Finally I got to the stage where I said, 'What the Hell! If I haven't got any talent, then there it is.' And I accepted the fact that I didn't have talent. Then, strangely enough, people started to say, 'You are not too bad. You should keep on acting.'

When you are anxious to get loud applause, you won't get it. But when you reach the state where it doesn't matter any longer, because you have accepted yourself and your own position, then people start to praise you. Maybe that is the secret of acting. The reason I managed to return to the Japanese stage with a fairly relaxed manner was that I knew, better than anyone else, that I had nothing special to offer, nothing particular with which to decorate the honour of my homecoming.

There is a particularly well-known section in *The Mahabharata* called the *Bhagavad Gita*. It occurs at the moment when the great warrior Arjuna is facing the climactic battle. He sees the faces of his uncles and cousins in the opposing camp, and recoils from the killing. The god Krishna talks to Arjuna for a long time, in order to persuade him to return to the battle. He says, 'The souls of human beings are eternal, but their bodies are merely temporary abodes. Therefore, even if you destroy your cousins' bodies, it does not mean that you have killed them. The most important thing is that you will have fulfilled your responsibilities' – which in Arjuna's case meant to act as a true warrior.

This is also the basis of the Buddhist philosophy of 'emptiness'. As the Hannya Shinkyo ('Heart sutra') says, 'All the material forms of the world are emptiness, yet emptiness is the form of the material world.'

An actor should 'act' in the same way. He or she has to be a good 'actor' in terms of human existence, not simply someone who works in the theatre. To be a good actor, you mustn't become lost in enjoying your action. Instead you should learn to see it, observe it, and then try to find the next step. Maybe one should act, knowing that the world is an illusion. If you think that because it is an illusion, you don't need to do anything, then that is not 'acting'. Knowing that action is an illusion, one must 'act' all the same.

Postscript

In January 1989, I found myself sitting in India, writing the last chapter of the Japanese version of this book. At long last I had arrived. The book was near its end, and I had finally come to India. When I was visiting Buddhist temples in Japan fifteen years before, I knew that eventually I wanted to search for my own roots in India. That wish was realised through my old friend Hugh McCormick, now Swami Ishwarananda.

The play of *The Mahabharata* was made into a film as the finale of the project, after we had returned from Japan. The nine-hour stage epic was condensed into a five-hour film, which was shown in cinemas and on television all over the world. The film was shot in an old studio in the suburbs of Paris, and during that period Ishwarananda suddenly turned up at the studio. He had come to Paris to attend lectures for the followers, and was only planning to stay one week. In his spare time, he wanted to see Peter Brook, and to encounter his version of *The Mahabharata*. Already four years had passed since our last reunion. Now the costume of a swami fitted him quite naturally, and 'Hugh' had completely vanished. He had an air of dignity and confidence that was appropriate and becoming to 'Swami Ishwarananda'. He had truly become a Hindu priest.

After he left the studio, I sat in a corner, hidden among the props. Tears gushed endlessly down my face, making me worried that my make-up for the part of an eighty-year-old man might be spoiled. I did not understand the reason for those tears. Was it perhaps that I was pleased to see him become a worthy monk? No, not that. In the last fifteen years, he has found his own direction. Now he is pursuing his path with absolute certainty, and seeing the fruits of past effort. Compared to this, what a miserable mess I had made of my own life! Around the period when I first met Hugh, I had a feeling that I had found something for myself. After that shortlived certainty, I continued drifting from place to place. I still didn't know where to settle myself. I was ashamed of my wretched, desultory self. What had I been doing in the last twenty years since I had left Japan? Wandering round the world! What had I built? Nothing! Even now, I am still drifting around, exactly as I was twenty years ago. What was the aim behind my initial departure? Surely it wasn't merely a flight from Japanese society?

During the sixties and seventies, many young people left their own countries and began to travel. Quite a few headed to India in search of a new way of thinking, while others established self-contained communities in remote places. A section of Japanese youth did the same. A number of us had gone abroad at the time of the anti-American–Japanese treaty demonstrations, around 1970. Probably Hugh and I were both part of these movements. More than twenty years have passed since then. Some of those who left their own societies have now built up a firm base in their new world, like Hugh. Some became disillusioned. Others viewed it as a pleasant part of their youthful experience, and have now gone back to working in the mainstream of their own society. However, I am still alone, still unable to choose any of these options, still drifting.

I wanted to confide these frustrations of mine to Ishwarananda, and arranged to meet him at one of the cafés in the Marais district. I grumbled for a long time. Ishwarananda listened to me very attentively, then said, 'How about going back to Japan? But before you do, you should come and have a break at Mukutananda's ashram, in Bombay. I will be there, helping the number two guru, Gurumai, so I'll be able to look after you. I would recommend a month's break there.'

I accepted the invitation immediately.

This would not be my first visit to India. At the beginning of 1985, Brook's company had made a special two-week visit to India, as a part of the research for *The Mahabharata*. We had travelled towards the south from Bombay, in order to study the various art forms which dealt with the story of *The Mahabharata*. We had also visited a famous guru, and asked him about the text. I felt that if there were such a thing as the 'birthplace of humanity', India would be an ideal candidate. We ate Indian curry with our fingers. I liked that. The food was appreciated by the eyes, savoured by the fingers, and then tasted by the mouth. I had many extraordinary experiences during the tour, but the most striking moment occurred in Benares.

Benares is a Hindu sacred place, which has been a religious centre since around 800 BC. People come here to purify their bodies in the holy river Ganges, and burn the corpses of their families on the riverbanks. It is said that if the ashes and bones are thrown into the Ganges, the person's spirit will attain Nirvana, and will no longer need to be reincarnated on Earth. Therefore, many Hindu believers, whose lives are nearing their ends, come to live in this town. They wish to die here. At dawn and at sunset, you can see many people along the banks of the river, pouring water on their bodies, purifying their mouths, and sitting down to meditate. I watched this scene from a boat. As the sun set, the riverbank grew darker. Then the corpses were placed on funeral pyres and the flames from the burning timbers and bodies lit the riverside. When I looked more closely, I noticed the families of the dead, watching the body burning away. From the distance of the boat, those figures looked like mushrooms on the earth. No individual figure was visible on the riverbank as the sun vanished. They looked like a single herd.

'Yes, it's true. The individual does not really exist. We are merely a part of that "mushroom herd". When we die, the body will be thrown into that fire, and in its place, a new mushroom will emerge. Living and being burnt. Being burnt and living again.'

I felt as if I was seeing reincarnation in front of my own eyes. The flow of the river Ganges was very calm, and I looked on that endlessly moving, still water. Beyond the water, the earth of the riverbank spread. The body became fire, and the smoke was carried upwards by the wind, until it disappeared into the sky. The five elements of Buddhism (heaven, air, fire, earth, water) seemed, at that moment, to be the mere reflection of a living reality. They were no longer concepts from a profound Buddhist philosophy.

As I promised Ishwarananda, I arrived at Bombay airport. After a two-hour drive in a taxi, I reached the ashram. When I arrived, just before midday, a chorus of chanted mantras could be heard coming from the interior of the building. Twenty years ago, Western hippies first came to India, but I had arrived after a long period of wandering. I dragged my body, weary from its long journeying, to the gate of the ashram. The sun was dazzling. There was a flower shop beside the gate where you could buy garlands to offer to the guru. I stopped and contemplated whether or not I should go in.

'I have come all this way. I might as well go in.'

And so I persuaded myself. I began to pass through the gate.